Dimensions of Effective Counseling:

*Cognitive flexibility and psychological openness
in counselor selection*

MERRILL'S INTERNATIONAL SERIES
IN EDUCATION

Under the Editorship of Kimball Wiles,
late Dean of the College of Education, University of Florida, and Walter B. Waetjen,
Associate Editor, University of Maryland.

EXPLORATIONS IN COUNSELING
SERIES

John M. Whiteley, Editor, Washington
University, St. Louis.

DIMENSIONS
OF
EFFECTIVE COUNSELING:

*Cognitive flexibility and psychological openness
in counselor selection*

THOMAS W. ALLEN
and
JOHN M. WHITELEY

Washington University

In Collaboration with
NORMAN A. SPRINTHALL
RALPH L. MOSHER
ROLLA T. DONAGHY
Harvard University

CHARLES E. MERRILL PUBLISHING CO.
COLUMBUS, OHIO
A Bell & Howell Company

Library of Congress Catalog Number 68-24462

1 2 3 4 5 6 7 8 9 10—74 73 72 71 70 69 68

PRINTED IN THE UNITED STATES OF AMERICA

DEDICATION

To Marlys and Shirley

PREFACE

The most obvious audience for this book is the counselor educator for his is the difficult task of selecting students for training. But the implications of cognitive flexibility and psychological openness extend far beyond. For instance, the selection strategy which is articulated and tested here has clear relevance to other attempts to understand effective human beings—whether the purpose is selection or some sort of clinical intervention.

For the practitioner in the field, the attempt has been to elaborate a theoretical structure related to operational behaviors in counseling which have relevance to work with normal human beings in primarily educational settings at the elementary, secondary, and college levels.

To the student struggling to master the difficult art of counseling, the presentation is in terms of what the counselor is to *do* rather than some abstract conceptualization of what he *is*.

It is the task of this book to describe cognitive flexibility and psychological openness, to articulate the theoretical context from which they arise and to which they are related and, finally, to offer experimental evidence to support their use in counselor selection.

Our concern is with effectiveness in counseling. Cognitive flexibility and psychological openness have been conceptualized as important dimensions in effective counseling behavior, though by no means the only relevant variable for effective counseling. Both are viewed as the sources of important counseling skills. Certain desirable counselor behaviors tend to flow from flexibility and openness. Conversely, a number of clearly undesirable counselor behaviors are derived from cognitive rigidity and psychological closedness.

Cognitive Flexibility

Cognitive flexibility is the capacity to think and act simultaneously and appropriately in a given situation. It refers to dimensions of openmindedness, adaptability, and a resistance to premature closure in perception and cognition. Rigidity assumes the opposite, an intolerance of ambiguity or an excessive need for structure.

Effective counselor behavior results from the ability to remain cognitively flexible; to respond, for example, to both the content and feeling which the client communicates. The implication is that the rigid counselor, unable to respond to the demands of the interaction with the client, construes the situation without reference to the client. This might take the form of seeking early closure on the client's problems and systematically "tuning out" additional responses by the client. Flexible behavior, in contrast, would imply a general avoidance of either excessive structuring in the counseling situation, or the complete ambiguity of nondirection.

Though the dimension of flexibility-rigidity has long been a topic of considerable interest to psychologists, the bulk of the research has been concerned with pathology.[1] Consequently, relatively little consideration has been given to the relevance of the concept of cognitive flexibility to education and to its implications for working with the normal personality.

Thus, working with cognitive flexibility in teaching behavior (Chapter 2) and in counselor behavior (Chapters 3 and 4) must be regarded as an initial attempt to change the focus from pathology, and rest it squarely on problems confronted in selecting from among normal people to train for professional counseling roles in educational settings.

Psychological Openness

Rokeach (1960) uses "openness" as a term to refer to the extensiveness of communication between various parts of a system. He suggests that it is a significant dimension of human personality. To extend Rokeach's terminology, the "open

---

[1] Three very different approaches have dominated the research efforts. Many early studies (Goldstein and Scheerer, 1941; Kounin, 1941; Werner, 1946) confined themselves to inferring rigidity based upon simple motor or perceptual factors and the samples were primarily of brain damaged, sub-normal, or psychotic persons.

A second theme in the literature is composed of the factor analytic studies which have focused on whether rigidity is a general trait. Adorno (1950), Cowan and Thompson (1951), Murphy (1951), Wesley (1953), and Johnson and Stern (1955) have been leading exponents of the theory that rigidity is a general factor in personality. As Adorno (1950) stated, there is a:

> correspondence in the type of approach in outlook a subject is likely to have in a great variety of areas, ranging from the most intimate features of family and sex adjustments through relationships with other people in general, to religion and to social and political philosophy. (p. 589)

Critical comment has abounded in regard to this general trait approach. Wolpert (1955), Pitcher and Stacey (1954), Schaie (1955), Scheier and Ferguson (1952), Fisher (1950), Goodstein (1953), Luchins (1949), and Applezweig (1954) have all questioned the existence of this general rigidity syndrome. As stated by Fisher (1950), "the concept of general rigidity as a real entity is to a considerable degree fictitious . . ." Goodstein (1953) concluded that:

> The review of the literature inevitably leads to the conclusion that no overall or general trait of rigidity can be behaviorably demonstrated. (p. 350)

The third current is a dynamic approach (Eriksen and Einstein, 1953; Cowan, 1952; Brown, 1953) which has viewed rigidity in general terms as a defense or the result of defenses mobilized to minimize anxiety.

These studies constitute a detailed presentation of the different approaches.

person" is one in whom there is a relatively high degree of self-communication. The "closed person" is one in whom there is a greater amount of isolation among the various levels and/or varieties of experience. Thus, the placement of an individual on a continuum from psychological openness to psychological closedness is determined by the degree of self-awareness he has, the awareness of his own feelings, yearnings, impulses, and imaginings.

The importance of psychological openness as a principle of personality organization has been most fully realized by workers in "creativity" (Barron, 1963; Bruner, 1962; Getzels and Jackson, 1962; Rogers, 1961). However, there is a good deal of theoretical and experimental support for the notion that psychological openness is an important prerequisite for counseling practice. There are two general arguments.

First, it is maintained that psychological openness is an essential precondition to the understanding of the thoughts and feelings of other people. Freud's observation that a counselor's lack of insight into his own pyschological processes is an important source of distortion in his perception of clients has been endorsed by writers outside the analytic tradition, for example, Rogers (1951) and Tyler (1961), as well as those within it; Fenichel (1945) and Knight (1953).

Further theoretical considerations strongly suggest that psychological openness makes an important positive contribution to a counselor's understanding of his client. It appears to many theorists that a counselor's own feelings are important sources of information in the process of unraveling the emotional communications of others. (Bakan 1956, Bordin 1955, Katz 1963, and Schafer 1959).

The second argument is that the psychological openness of the counselor is an essential factor in the establishment of an interpersonal atmosphere conducive to client exploration. This contention rests heavily upon the work of Carl Rogers and Sidney Jourard. Rogers (1957) asserts that the openness of the counselor to his own feelings ("congruence") is one of the "necessary and sufficient conditions of therapeutic personality change." Similarly, Jourard (1964) posits a "dyadic effect" in counseling. That is, the extent to which clients are able to risk self-recognition seems to be related to the willingness of counselors to take the same risk.

Psychological openness has been developed as a construct in psychological theory in Chapter 5. Based on the theoretical underpinnings, a series of operational definitions were specified (Chapter 6) and applied to the problem of identifying effective counselors (Chapter 7). As with the parallel development of cognitive flexibility, the problem which this work confronts is that of selecting from among normal people to train for professional counseling roles in educational settings.

REFERENCES

Adorno, T., et al. The Authoritarian Personality. New York: Harper & Row, Publishers, 1950.

Applezweig, D., "Some determinants of behavioral rigidity," Journal of Abnormal and Social Psychology, 49, 1954, 224-228.

Bakan, D., "Clinical psychology and logic," American Psychologist, 11, 1956, 655-662.

Barron, F., Creativity and Psychological Health. Princeton, N.J.: Van Nostrand, 1963.

Bordin, E. S., Psychological Counseling. New York: Appleton-Century-Crofts, 1955.

Brown, R. W., "A determinant of the relationship between rigidity and authoritarianism," Journal of Abnormal and Social Psychology, 48, 1953, 474-475.

Bruner, J., "The conditions of creativity." In H. E. Gruber, G. Tenell, and M. Wertheimer (eds.), Contemporary Approaches to Creative Thinking. New York: Atherton Press, 1962, 1-30.

Cowen, E. L., "The influence of varying degrees of psychological stress on problem solving behavior," Journal of Abnormal and Social Psychology, 47, 1952, 512-519.

Cowen, E. L., G. G. Thompson. "Problem solving rigidity and personality structure," Journal of Abnormal and Social Psychology, 46, 1951, 165-176.

Ericksen, C. W., D. Eisenstein. "Perceptual rigidity and the rorschach," Journal of Personality, 21, 1953, 386-391.

Fenichel, O., The Psychoanalytic Theory of Neurosis. New York: W. W. Norton and Company, 1945.

Fisher, S., "Patterns of personality rigidity and some of their determinants," Psychological Monographs, Vol. 64, 1950.

Getzels, J., and P. Jackson. Creativity and Intelligence. New York: John Wiley and Sons, Inc., 1962.

Goldstein, K. and M. Scheerer. "Abstract and concrete behavior: an experimental study with special tests," Psychological Monograph, 53, 1941, No. 239.

Goodstein, L., "Intellectual rigidity and social attitudes," Journal of Abnormal and Social Psychology, 48, 1953, 345-353.

Johnson, L. C., J. A. Stern. "Rigidity on the Rorschach and response to intermittent photic stimulation," Journal of Consulting Psychology, 19, 1955, 311-317.

Jourard, S. M., The Transparent Self. New York: Van Nostrand, 1964.

Katz, R. L., Empathy: Its Nature and Uses. New York: Free Press of Glencoe, 1963.

Knight, R. P., "The present status of organized psycho-analysis in the United States," American Journal of Psychoanalysis, 1, 1953, 197.

Luchins, A. S., "Rigidity and ethnocentrism: a critique," Journal of Personality, 17, 1949, 449-466.

Murphy, G., An Introduction to Psychology. New York: Harper & Row, Publishers, 1951.

Pitcher, B., and C. Stacey. "Is einstellung rigidity a general trait?" Journal of Abnormal and Social Psychology, 49, 1954, 3-6.

Rogers, C. R., Client-centered Therapy. Boston: Houghton-Mifflin Company, 1951.

Rogers, C. R., "Necessary and sufficient conditions of therapeutic personality change," Journal of Consulting Psychology, 21, 1957, 95-103.

Schafer, R., "Generative empathy in the treatment situation," Psychoanalytic Quarterly, 28, 1959, 342-373.

Schaie, K., "A test of behavioral rigidity," Journal of Abnormal and Social Psychology, 51, 1955, 604-610.

Scheier, I., and G. Ferguson. "Further factorial studies of tests of rigidity," Canadian Journal of Psychology, 6, 1952, 18-30.

Tyler, L. E., The Work of the Counselor (2nd ed.). New York: Appleton-Century-Crofts, 1961.

Werner, H., "Abnormal and subnormal rigidity," Journal of Abnormal and Social Psychology, 41, 1946, 15-24.

Wesley, E., "Perseverative behavior in a concept-formation task as a function of manifest anxiety and rigidity," Journal of Abnormal and Social Psychology, 48, 1953, 129.

Wolpert, E., "A new view of rigidity," Journal of Abnormal and Social Psychology, 51, 1955, 589-594.

ACKNOWLEDGMENTS

We wish to express our gratitude to the following professional publications for allowing us to reprint portions of articles which have previously appeared in their pages.

Allen, "Effectiveness of counselor trainees as a function of psychological openness," *Journal of Counseling Psychology, 14,* 1967, 35-40.

Emlaw, Mosher, Sprinthall, Whiteley, "Teacher Effectiveness: A method for prediction and evaluation," *National Elementary Principal, 43,* 1963, 38-49. Copyright 1963, Department of Elementary School Principals, National Education Association. All rights reserved.

Sprinthall, Whiteley, Mosher. "A study of teacher effectiveness," *The Journal of Teacher Education, 17,* 1966, 93-106.

Sprinthall, Whiteley, Mosher, "Cognitive flexibility as a dimension of counselor behavior: Definition, rationale, research focus." *Counselor Education and Supervision, 5,* 1966, 188-197.

Whiteley, Sprinthall, Mosher, Donaghy. "Selection and evaluation of counselor effectiveness," *Journal of Counseling Psychology, 14,* 1967, 226-234. Copyright 1954 by the American Psychological Association and reproduced by permission.

The freedom to work within a university community is generally the result of considerable personal and administrative support from a number of individuals. Our freedom to pursue these studies is in large part the result of the efforts of Carl A. Dauten, Judson T. Shaplin, and Dyckman W. Vermilye of Washington University, and Dana Farnsworth, Charles McArthur, David Tiedeman, and Theodore Sizer of Harvard University. We gratefully acknowledge their support.

Preparing a manuscript through its various drafts is a laborious undertaking. The task was cheerfully and competently borne by Judy Cohen, Janet Lombardo, Carole Kaye, Judy Platt, and Carol Zeidman. We gratefully appreciate their efforts. Also, Kay Garrett of Charles E. Merrill has given generously of her time in the editorial and production aspects of final preparation.

Finally, our wives understandingly tolerated the extra hours their husbands spent in dens and libraries as part of this undertaking. Our indebtedness to them can only be partially reflected in the dedication of this book.

T.W.A.
J.M.W.

St. Louis, Missouri
May, 1968

Table of Contents

Dimensions of Effective Counseling:

Cognitive flexibility and psychological openness in counselor selection

SECTION I

INTRODUCTION

1

Introduction to the Problem
of Selecting Counselors

And whatever one may think of the narrowness of the mind-curers, their logical position is impregnable. They are proving by the most brilliant new results that the therapeutic relation may be what we can at present describe only as the relation of one person to another person; and they are consistent in resisting to the ultimate any legislation that would make "examinable" information the root of medical virtue, and hamper the free play of personal force and affinity by mechanically imposed conditions (William James in a letter to the *Boston Evening Transcript,* March 24, 1894; cited by Gay Wilson Allen, 1967, p. 372.).

This heretical asseveration of James apparently did considerable damage to his standing in the eyes of the professional community. However, it clearly squares with the testimony of common sense. It is widely recognized that some persons are apparently by virtue of their personal qualities alone more helpful to their fellows in moments of personal stress than other equally well-intentioned people. Indeed, it would seem that whenever we come across such a person, a person with whom we like to share our own puzzlement, anxiety, or despair, we often find that a number of other people share our sentiment. Something in the person seems to speak meaningfully to the confusion and distress of others.

This belief has a corollary lodged deep in the prevailing views of counseling. It is the proposition that the personality of the counselor, the kind of human being he is, is a prepotent factor in the determination of his professional competence.

Carl Rogers, for example, is particularly articulate in this regard. He asserts that the qualities of the counseling relationship which seem to be most closely associated with progress "are not constituted of technical or ideological sophistication. They are personal human qualities—something the counselor experiences, not something he knows" (Rogers, 1962, p. 428). In a similar vein, Kell and Mueller (1966) find evidence in their study of the interaction process in counseling that the needs of the counselor as a person have substantial effects on the progress of the client. They aver that "counselors help their clients by being

3

human" (p. 65). Izette de Forest, an interpreter of Ferenczi, has much the same insight. For her, whatever the counselor is able to do for the client is principally the result of the kind of person he is. Patterson (1959) contends that the personality of the counselor is the basic ingredient in counseling and that "academic training or information has little if any influence on this personality" (p. 14). Hahn and MacLean (1955) argue that acceptance to a counseling program should be highly provisional as it takes time to assess the nature of a candidate's personality. This vital factor in the making of a counselor must be given heavy weight in determining his suitability for the profession (p. 16). The list of similar statements continues indefinitely and includes representatives from virtually all schools of thought. The results of Fiedler's inevitably cited studies (1950a; 1950b) are illustrative of the degree of consensus which seems to exist in regard to the importance of counselor personality.

Several recent studies offer some empirical support for this contention. Bergin (1963), for example, in dealing with the fact that positive change is often found in the personalities of the members of "control groups" in studies of counseling outcome, notes that persons selected for these groups (those not selected for formal counseling) very frequently seek help elsewhere (Frank, 1961). They turn, most generally, to people who are outside the orthodox "mental health professions" (Gurin, Veroff, and Feld, 1960). That these "controls" do then change in a positive direction to a degree as significant as that found in those subjects in treatment with certified professionals suggests that it is *not* the specialized training of the latter which accounts for the improvement of their clientele. Rather, it appears, some quality of personality which appears in professionals and nonprofessionals alike must be responsible. Therefore, Bergin concludes that counselors "who produce positive results are those who have certain personal qualities and ways of responding to others rather than a well-trained armanetarium of techniques" (1963, p. 248).

Luborsky (1950; 1952) found a constancy between the quality of the day-to-day relationships of psychiatric residents and their therapeutic relations. Parloff (1956) reports similar findings. Ellsworth (1962) found an appreciable degree of consistency in feeling-verbalization to be characteristic of 22 counselor trainees. That is, the degree to which a trainee tended to respond in terms of feelings in a noncounseling situation was found to be a reliable indicator of the degree to which he would respond to client feelings. These data suggest that counseling is, as Patterson and others have indicated, in the final analysis an expression of the counselor's personality.

Sheehan (1953) reports the results of a study of 21 clients and their counselors. The change in the clients over counseling appeared to be directly related to the

---

[1] C. H. Patterson's paper in the first volume of this series presents what is, perhaps, the most thorough review of recent developments in the theory and research addressed to this problem. Consequently, an exhaustive treatment of this material will not be attempted here.

nature of the counselor's personality. Sheehan states that "the extent of shift (in the client) appears (to be a function) primarily of therapist personality independent of his theoretical predilection and *modus operandi*" (Sheehan, 1953, p. 434). Similarly, Whitehorn and Betz (1954; 1960) found that it was possible to distinguish successful therapists from less successful ones in terms of personality constellations as expressed in their interests and personal preferences.

Further support for this notion is to be garnered from the investigations of the psychotherapy research group at Wisconsin under the leadership of Carl Rogers. These studies employed carefully matched experimental and control groups and multiple outcome criteria which had been carefully examined in prior work. They found that clients who showed progress in counseling tended to cluster around certain counselors and that those who failed to progress or who regressed clustered around certain others. When notice is taken of the homogeneity of the group of counselors involved in terms of technical training and experience, the significance of counselor personality factors seems to become more evident (Truax, 1963). What is more, Carkhuff and Truax (1966) found a number of other important outcome studies are amenable to similar analysis.

Nevertheless, despite the general unanimity of expert opinion and the growing volume of supportive research indicating that the personality of the counselor is a crucial consideration, a survey of the "practices in counselor trainee selection" employed by various training centers reveals that the emphasis falls almost exclusively on academic factors (American Psychological Association, 1954). The reason for this is not difficult to ascertain. Selection is more than a matter of believing that personality factors are important; it involves the specification and measurement of these factors. Herein lies the difficulty. As Hill notes, though there are "many pronouncements regarding the personal characteristics and the competencies needed by guidance and personnel workers . . . little of this literature may be said to be based on research . . ." (1961, p. 57).

Barry and Wolf (1958) surveyed the *Personnel and Guidance Journal* and found that only 14 of its 411 articles dealt with any aspect of "counselor training." Of the 136 articles based on research, only two were concerned with counselor training (Barry and Wolf, 1958). The literature seems to consist in the main, of a priori lists of assorted virtues which might be sought in candidates for any profession. Cox (1945) asks for some 24 characteristics in prospective counselors. His list includes such things as "fairness," "sincerity," "personality," "good character," and "wholesome philosophy." Graves (1944) suggests "integrity, vitality, judgment, health, industriousness, high personal standards, adaptability, training, and experience." Bowler and Dawson (1948) seek "objectivity, respect for the individual, self-understanding, mature judgment, ability to listen and keep confidences, resourcefulness and reliability, sense of humor, constructive criticism, and personal integrity."

Obviously, as Jones (1951) points out, such attempts, based entirely on subjectivity and without operational specifications, are "very unsatisfactory."

Although the American Psychological Association survey (1954) found that less than half of the counselor training institutions studied were satisfied that they knew what personality variables to assess and frankly recognized this to be a serious problem, almost no research relevant to it is available.

Neither has the research which has been done been of much assistance. One line of investigation has attempted to determine the type of people that counselors are (Cottle and Lewis, 1954; Cottle, Lewis, and Penney, 1954; Cottle and Wands, 1955; Cottle, Pownall, and Steimel, 1955). Personality scales such as the Minnesota Multiphasic Personality Inventory (MMPI) and the Guilford-Zimmerman Temperament Survey (GZTS) were administered to groups of counselors and teachers. Item analyses revealed the nature of the items which discriminated counselors from teachers. However, since no measure of competence in counseling was included, this research is of little, if any, utility in the selection of counselors or the understanding of counseling effectiveness.

Arbuckle (1956) employed sociometric choice as a criterion in studying a group of 70 counselor trainees. The trainees were asked to list the three of their number from whom they themselves would be most likely to seek counseling, and conversely, the three from whom they would be least likely to seek counseling. An examination of the MMPI, Heston, and Kuder protocols for the six most frequently chosen and six most frequently rejected trainees was made and the differentiating items noted. The most popular trainees were found to be generally better adjusted. This study lacks any theoretical underpinning and requires replication before any conclusions can be drawn from it. Furthermore, the relationship between sociometric selection and actual performance in counseling remains obscure.

Brams (1957; 1961) failed to confirm these results. He found the effectiveness of counselors' communications to be unrelated to standard personality inventories. Campbell (1962), likewise, found no relationship between the interview behavior of 24 students in a counseling psychology practicum, defined in terms of Danskin's (1953) subroles, and their performance on the Guilford-Zimmerman Temperament Survey and the Kuder.

Similarly, Abeles (1958) was unable to predict supervisors' judgments of counselor promise from paper-and-pencil estimates of adjustment. Rather, his results suggest another set of discriminating variables.

Stefflre, King, and Leafgren (1962), like Arbuckle, compared the results of a similar test battery for participants in an NDEA counseling institute with peer ratings. The results suggest still other isolated factors to distinguish among effective and ineffective counselors. Consequently, since each application of these measures tends to produce, *post hoc*, a new group of differentia, it appears that little confidence can be placed in them for predictive selection purposes.

Dole (1964) presents the findings from a major study of this sort. A wide range of standard psychometric instruments was employed and supplemented by a number of tests devised especially for the purpose. The battery was applied to 92 teachers enrolled in a school-counseling workshop. This sample was divided randomly. The criterion, "effectiveness in school counseling," was assessed by means of ratings made by the guidance faculty, the state supervisors of guidance, and the principals under whom they worked. The latter ratings were made some six months after initial employment.

The investigators divided the sample randomly and examined the data for one-half of it. They adjusted their scoring systems so that the tests predicted the criterion ratings most effectively for that part of the sample and then applied the revised scoring procedures to the remaining subjects. Further cross-validation was attempted with 29 enrollees in a summer NDEA institute and 30 enrollees in a year-long institute. Only one of the extensive number of measures tried was successful in predicting more than one set of ratings for more than a single sample beyond a chance level. All of the others disappeared in cross-validation. The single survivor was "counselor potential," a set of ratings made by the principals who had employed the students as teachers prior to their entrance into counseling. It correlated significantly with principals' ratings for the first two samples, with state supervisors' ratings for one of three samples, and with faculty ratings for one of two samples. It is interesting to note that none of the three groups of raters agreed significantly with any other group.

Similar efforts have been made in related fields. Kelly and Fiske (1951) attempted to predict the performance of students in clinical psychology. Virtually the entire arsenal of major tests of personality was employed. Though the instruments were in the hands of some leading psychologists, the predictive validities were modest indeed. Further, the tests which emerged as relatively superior predictors in regard to the first sample did not stand up on cross-validation.

Snyder (1955) had instructors in the clinical psychology program of the Pennsylvania State University rate 423 students in terms of competence. The contingency coefficients computed as indices of agreement among the four judges were in the .60's and significant beyond the 1 per cent level. Snyder subsequently attempted to differentiate between the "good" or "poor" clinical trainees by means of an item analysis of the Minnesota Multiphasic Personality Inventory. However, this attempt was unsuccessful. Snyder was unable to build an empirical scale to predict clinical competence by these means.

It appears that a major source of the difficulty with the foregoing studies may be the "trait approach" or, in Stern, Stein, and Bloom's (1956) terms, the "empirical approach," which they use. Proceeding without benefit of specific predictions drawn from well-articulated theories, the investigators attempt to identify individual elements of personality related to counseling behavior.

They seemed to assume that since there appear to be differences in personality between "good" and "poor" counselors, it was necessary only to administer the standard personality tests and tabulate the differences.

However, the falaciousness of this approach is readily discernible. In the first place, it is clear that no existing test of personality is a satisfactory measure of personality as a whole. Hence, it cannot be anticipated that tests will inevitably discriminate between levels of competence in counseling simply because they are the "standard tests." The direction of theory is required. In the second place, it is doubtful that "good" and "poor" counselors may be distinguished in terms of specifiable aggregates of individual personality traits. Tyler (1961), for example, argues forcefully that there is no single personality type, no single profile of personality trait values, to be sought in prospective counselors. She contends that counselors may arrive at similar goals by different approaches. That is, counselors with dissimilar personalities may approach the same client in different ways with equally favorable results. She writes,

> Perhaps it would be better if we all assumed that any personality pattern which permits rich and deep relationships with other human beings to develop is satisfactory (1961, p. 246).

Therein, however, lies the crux of the matter.

An Alternate Research Strategy

The sterility of the foregoing research does not invalidate the hypothesis that personality factors are important predictors of the effectiveness of counselors. But it does suggest that it is not sufficient to content oneself with casting results of whatever tests are available and or are conveniently gathered into the hopper to see if, perchance, some might covary appreciably. An alternative approach to the problem is called for.

It appears more promising to proceed according to some sort of understanding of the demands of the situation to which prediction is to be made and the range of capabilities which human beings have, at least potentially, available to them to meet these demands.

Symonds and Dudek (1956) employed this strategy to deal with the very similar problem of teacher selection. Rather than seeking one-to-one relationships between test factors and effectiveness in teaching according to the foregoing model, they made their predictions on the basis of higher order personality variables drawn from their theoretical understanding of the demands of teaching. That is, such dimensions as "personality organization" and "the capacity to relate to others" were identified from theory. Subsequently, they set out to assess the relative standing of each of their subjects on these dimensions. Attention was given to the degree to which the pattern of test scores in each case suggested a given construct instead of to the differences in individual scores. These investigators recognized that many different score patterns could convey the same meaning, *i.e.*, that a given construct could be indicated by a large variety of possible score patterns. Their results were promising. A rank order correlation of + .60 was achieved between the predictions of effectiveness in teaching generated in this manner and the independent ratings of the quality of the teacher's performances. "These correlations are considerably higher than anything hitherto reported in the literature on factors predictive of teacher success" (Symonds and Dudek, 1956, p. 228).

The results of Holt and Luborsky (1958) are likewise suggestive. Although success in psychiatry, the variable with which they were concerned, is probably not as closely related to successful counseling in an educational setting as is effective teaching (Sprinthall, Whiteley, and Mosher, 1965), there are nonetheless important points at which extrapolation is possible. Holt and Luborsky employed a wide range of clinical techniques to predict the level of performance of psychiatric residents. Forewarned by research in which the lack of predictive validity of clinical techniques could reasonably be attributed to the unfamiliarity of the participating clinicians with the criterion situation which they were predicting and by Meehl's (1954) caveat in regard to clinical prediction, these investigators began with an intensive analysis of the demands of psychiatry. They then tested their theories on a pilot group and adjusted their thinking in terms of their findings. Wherever possible, clinical judgment was supplemented by empirically derived regression equations.

Their results reveal uneven success. Two judges attempted to integrate the material at hand and predict the competence ratings to be given the residents. One judge did quite well; his ratings correlated +.57 with the criteria. However, the second judge managed to reach only the +.22 level. What is more, the validities present in this initial test disappeared in cross-validation (Holt and Luborsky, 1958).

One possible source of difficulty here may be the unreliability of the predictors. For example, Holt developed a manual for prediction from the Thematic Apperception Test. Though very promising in its initial trial use, the interscorer reliability stayed between +.23 and +.42 (Holt, 1958). Accordingly, validities shrank to negligible levels in cross-validation. Clearly, the relationship between the TAT behavior alluded to in the manual and performance in psychiatry would have to be an unimaginably powerful one to be discernible through the amount of error introduced by this degree of unreliability.

Summary and Conclusions

Writers from virtually every school of thought in counseling insist that the counselor as a person is the central determinant of the effectiveness of his counseling. Research tends to support this general contention. For example, Bergin (1963) suggests that the improvement of so-called "controls" in studies of the effects of counseling is the result of the fact that they have sought and found help in persons outside the mental health professions. The fact that these non-specialists are apparently of considerable assistance points up the contribution of nontechnical factors. This suggestion is supported by the findings of Truax (1963) and Carkhuff and Truax (1966). It was found that successful counseling cases tend to cluster around certain others whose technical and *professional* credentials are indistinguishable from those of the first group.

However, despite the burgeoning body of evidence in support of the general proposition that personality is crucial to the counselor's professional role, the selection of counselor trainees remains almost exclusively dependent upon the indications of academic promise which they present. This paradox is somewhat illumined by the fact that there seems to be little solid operational knowledge in regard to the specific personality characteristics essential to the counseling enterprise.

While there are many lists of desirable traits available, the traits are either so vague as to be untestable or so general as to lack discriminating power. The research that has been mounted is, in the main, characterized by attempts to determine what elements of test behavior discriminate between "good" and "poor" counselors. These efforts, which are, in general, atheoretical, tend to rely on the item analyses of standard personality inventories. Their harvest has been negligible. No stable list of reliable differentia has been experimentally certified.

The situation is very much the same as that in the related profession, teaching. Solemn admonitions and elaborate catalogues of requisite virtues abound. So, too, do efforts to separate "successful" candidates from their "unsuccessful" comrades. As in the case of counselor selection, this work has been little fruit. However, further research has taken a different and apparently more productive tack. Some researchers have abandoned the search for a definite set of low-level personality variables which will effectively discriminate between "good" and "poor" teachers. Higher-level personality variables relevant to teaching have been derived from theory. Assessment of these personality variables has proceeded with the realization that they may be represented by a wide range of item constellations, that they are not tied to any single set of test "signs." This strategy, although as yet sparingly employed, has met some success. A somewhat similar approach to the selection of psychiatric residents was less successful. However, it appears that, in this case, potentially promising results were lost due to the psychometric faults of the measures employed.

Thus, it seems that while there is a good deal of merit in Cattell's (1958) point that psychology is a bit top heavy, having a surfeit of elaborate theories and a dearth of reliable evidence concerning relationships among psychological phenomena, the atheoretical, bivariate studies which compose the bulk of the work on counselor personality are certainly on the lowest level of experimental inquiry. In most of these researches it is clear that most of the energy involved has been expended in the gathering and tabulation of data. There is little evidence of advance thought. Some studies have "tested" clinical conceptions, but have employed them in their most hackneyed form, e.g., Brams (1955). Others appear to be the result of throwing as many variables as possible into the hopper to see if, perchance, some of.them might not covary appreciably. The results have been of little utility. Indeed, even where positive findings are reported, e.g., Stefflre, King, and Leafgren (1962), there is considerable difficulty in interpreting their meaning, as these writers testify. Perhaps, then, it is more parsimonious to launch further research in this area from a more careful examination of the demands of the situation for which prediction is to be made. What follows is the product of such an assumption.

This book will present two theoretical structures, cognitive flexibility and psychological openness, which appear to be promising points of departure for the development of procedures (a) to anticipate the degree of success applicants to a counseling training program will have as counselors, and (b) to utilize more fully the resources of students accepted for training.

BIBLIOGRAPHY

Abeles, N. "A study of the characteristics of counselor trainees." Unpublished Doctoral Dissertation, University of Texas, 1958.

Allen, G. W. *William James*. New York: Viking, 1967.

American Psychological Association, Subcommittee on Counselor Trainee Selection, Counselor Training Committee, Division of Counseling Psychology. "An analysis of practices in counselor trainee selection," *Journal of Counseling Psychology, 1*, 1954, 174-179.

Arbuckle, D. S. "Client perception of counselor personality," *Journal of Counseling Psychology, 3*, 1956, 93-96.

Barry, R., and B. Wolf. "Five years of the *Personnel and Guidance Journal*," *36*, 1958, 549-556.

Bergin, A. E. "The effects of psychotherapy: negative results revisited," *Journal of Counseling Psychology, 10*, 1963, 244-249.

Bowler, E. M., and F. T. Dawson. *Counseling Employees*. New York: Prentice-Hall, 1948.

Brams, J. M. "An analysis of personality factors in counseling." Unpublished Doctoral Dissertation, University of Missouri, 1955.

Brams, J. M. "Counselor characteristics and effective communication in counseling," *Journal of Counseling Psychology, 8*, 1961, 25-30.

Campbell, R. E. "Counselor personality and background and his interview sub-role behavior," *Journal of Counseling Psychology, 9,* 1962, 329-334.

Carkhuff, R., and C. B. Truax "Toward explaining success and failure in inter-personal learning experiences," *Personnel and Guidance Journal, 44,* 1966, 723-728.

Cattell, R. B. "The dynamic calculus: A system of concepts derived from objec-tive motivation measurement," in *Assessment of Human Motives,* ed. G. Lindsey, New York: Holt, Rinehart, and Winston, 1958.

Cottle, W. C., and W. W. Lewis, Jr. "Personality characteristics of counselors; II. Male counselor responses to the MMPI and GZTS," *Journal of Coun-seling Psychology, 1,* 1954, 27-30.

Cottle, W. C., W. W. Lewis, Jr., and M. M. Penney. "Personal characteristics of counselors. III. An experimental attitude scale," *Journal of Counseling Psychology, 1,* 1954, 74-77.

Cottle, W. C., J. E. Pownall, and R. J. Steimel. "Counselors and teachers take the experimental attitude scale," *Personnel and Guidance Journal,* 1955, 374-378.

Cottle, W. C., and H. O. Wands. "High school counselors and teachers take the experimental attitude scale," *Journal of Counseling Psychology, 2,* 1955, 28-31.

Cox, R. D. *Counselors and Their Work.* Harrisburg: Archives Press, 1945

Danskin, D. B. "Roles played by counselors in their interviews," *Journal of Counseling Psychology, 2,* 1955, 22-27.

De Forest, I. *The Leaven of Love.* New York: Harper. 1960.

Dole, A. A. "The prediction of effectiveness in school counseling," *Journal of Counsulting Psychology, 11,* 1964, 112-121.

Ellsworth, S. "The consistency of counselor feeling-verbalization in and outside of the counselor-client relationship." Unpublished Doctoral Dissertation, Michigan State University, 1962.

Fiedler, R. E. "A comparison of therapeutic relationships in psychoanalytic, non-directive, and Adlerian psychotherapy," *Journal of Counseling Psycholo-gy, 14,* 1950a, 433-445.

Fiedler, R. E. "The concept of an ideal therapeutic relationship," *Journal of Counseling Psychology, 14,* 1950b, 239-245.

Frank, J. D. *Persuasion and Healing.* Baltimore: Johns Hopkins, 1961.

Graves, G. T. "The employee counselor," *Occupations,* 1944, 495-497.

Gurin, G., J. Veroff, and S. Feld. *Americans View Their Mental Health.* New York: Basic Books, 1960.

Hahn, M. E., and M. S. MacLean. *Counseling Psychology.* 2nd ed. New York: McGraw-Hill, 1955.

Hill, G. E. "The selection of school counselors," *Personnel and Guidance Jour-nal, 39,* 1961, 355-360.

Holt, R. R. "Formal aspects of the TAT: A neglected resource," *Journal of Projective Techniques, 22,* 1958, 163-172.

Holt, R. R., and L. L. Luborsky. *Personality Patterns of Psychiatrists: A Study of Methods for Selecting Residents.* I. New York: Basic Books, 1958.

Jones, A. J. *Principles of Guidance and Personnel Work*. New York: McGraw-Hill, 1951.

Kell, B. L., and W. J. Mueller. *Impact and Change: A Study of Counseling Relationships*. New York: Appleton-Century-Crofts, 1966.

Kelly, E. L., and D. W. Fiske. *The Prediction of Performance in Clinical Psychology*. Ann Arbor: University of Michigan Press, 1951.

Luborsky, L. L. "The personality of the psychotherapist," *Menninger Quarterly, 6,* 1952, 1-6.

Luborsky, L. L. "Selecting psychiatric residents: Survey of the Topeka research," *Bulletin of the Menninger Clinic, 18,* 1954, 252-269.

Meehl, P. E. "Comment on McArthur," *Journal of Counseling Psychology, 1,* 1954, 207-208.

Parloff, M. B. "Some factors affecting the quality of therapeutic relationships," *Journal of Abnormal Psychology, 52,* 1956, 5-10.

Patterson, C. H. *Counseling and Psychotherapy: Theory and Practice*. New York: Harpers, 1959.

Rogers, C. R. "The interpersonal relationship: The core of guidance," *Harvard Educational Review, 32,* 1962, 416-429.

Sheehan, J. C. "Rorschach changes during psychotherapy in relation to the personality of the therapist," *American Psychologist, 8,* 1953, 434.

Snyder, W. U. "The personality of clinical students," *Journal of Counseling Psychology, 2,* 1955, 47-52.

Sprinthall, N. A., J. M. Whiteley, and R. L. Mosher. *Cognitive Flexibility as a Dimension of Counselor Behavior: Definition, Rationale, Research Focus*. Cambridge, Mass.: Harvard University (mimeo), 1965.

Stefflre, B., P. King, and F. Leafgren. "Characteristics of counselors judged effective by their peers," *Journal of Counseling Psychology, 9,* 1962, 335-340.

Stern, G., M. Stein, and B. Bloom. *Methods in Personality Assessment*. Glencoe, Ill.: Free Press, 1956.

Symonds, P. M., and S. Z. Dudek. "Use of the Rorschach in the diagnosis of teacher effectiveness," *Journal of Projective Techniques and Personality Assessment, 20,* 1956, 227-234.

Truax, C. B. "Effective ingredients in psychotherapy: An approach to unraveling the patient-therapist interaction," *Journal of Counseling Psychology, 10,* 1963, 256-263.

Tyler, L. E. *The Work of the Counselor*. 2nd ed. New York: Appleton-Century-Crofts, 1961.

Whitehorn, J. C., and B. J. Betz. "A study of psychotherapeutic relationships between physicians and schizophrenic patients," *American Journal of Psychiatry, 111,* 1954, 321-331.

Whitehorn, J. C., and B. J. Betz. "Further studies of the doctor as a crucial variable in the outcome of treatment with schizophrenic patients," *American Journal of Psychiatry, 117,* 1960, 215-223.

SECTION II

COGNITIVE FLEXIBILITY AS A DIMENSION OF SELECTING COUNSELORS

2

A Study of Teacher Effectiveness: The Translation of Cognitive Flexibility Theory into Observable Human Behavior

Before proceeding with the translation of cognitive flexibility theory into counselor behavior, a parallel study of teacher effectiveness using cognitive flexibility as a construct for evaluating observable behavior in the classroom will be presented.

The purpose of this chapter is to apply the theory of flexibility-rigidity to an important educational problem, the prediction and evaluation of teacher effectiveness. Cognitive flexibility has been conceptualized as an important dimension in teacher effectiveness, though by no means the only relevant variable for effective teaching.

Research problems in teacher effectiveness provide an analogue to understanding problems in counseling research. For example, the lack of any well-defined criteria for teaching effectiveness (outcome in terms of how much the students actually learn) finds a parallel in the lack of an ultimate criterion in counseling or psychotherapy. Teaching research is currently moving toward the use of proximate criteria (Howsam, 1963). "Since it is not presently feasible to rely on the ultimate criterion of teacher effectiveness, it becomes necessary to attempt to develop intermediate or proximate criteria" (Howsam, 1963, p. 16). Howsam notes that this approach may well be a marked improvement because the focus is on what teachers do rather than what they are. In the next chapter a similar conceptualization will be utilized with regard to counseling.

Research on Teacher Effectiveness

The field of education has proven remarkably resistant to the application of scientific knowledge and the development of truly professional personnel (Howsam, 1963). Nowhere is this more in evidence than in the general area of research in teaching, and, more specifically, in teacher effectiveness. Existing research has a long but disappointing history.

The literature on teacher effectiveness is extensive (Domas and Tiedeman, 1950; Morsh and Wilder, 1954). There is little conclusive research, however, as to the conceptual issue of what (effective) teaching is, and the empirical problems of how effective teaching can be reliably predicted or measured. With few exceptions, research attempts to correlate measures of teacher attitudes or values, adjustment, needs, personality factors, and intelligence with ratings of teaching effectiveness have not produced significant results (Getzels and Jackson, 1964). The same is true for correlations of the teacher's cultural background, socio-economic status, sex, and marital status with ratings of effectiveness (Fattu, 1963). In short, "We do not know how to define, prepare for, or measure teacher competence" (Biddle, 1964, p. 3).

In the literature on teacher effectiveness there are a few studies which bear on the theoretical framework of this research: cognitive flexibility. Cognitive factors other than general intelligence have been little studied among teachers. Knoell (1953), however, found correlations ranging from .28 to .46 between two (of nine) measures of "ideational fluency" and careful ratings, *a year later,* of teaching effectiveness. Ideational fluency has been defined as a divergent thinking factor: "the ability to call up many ideas in a situation relatively free from restrictions where the quality of response is unimportant" (Guilford, 1959, p. 382). For example, one of the four-minute tests Knoell used required the subject to "write all the adjectives which could be used to describe a house," the other to "list all the things that are round or could be called round." The Knoell study, while essentially unique in the literature, appears relevant to the theoretical premise of the present investigation.

At a more general level, Goodlad (1959) has suggested that flexible teacher behavior is most relevant to effective classroom performance. "The right decision at the right moment is the essence of good teaching . . . [The teacher] must decide when to begin an activity and when to bring it to a close; when to use a student interest and when to pass it by; when to insist on exactness and when to sacrifice exactness to feeling. All these things and more the teacher must take into account in timing and pacing students' learning" (Goodlad, 1959, p. 39).

Ryans' Teacher Characteristics Study suggests that patterns of teaching behavior may be differentiated, and that certain patterns are significantly weighted by cognitive ability and/or attitudinal correlates of cognitive ability (Ryans, 1960). The relationship of such cognitive variables to ratings of teaching effectiveness, however, was by no means conclusively answered by Ryans' study.

Anderson and Hunka (1963) have extensively documented the theoretical rationale as well as the existing research evidence on the concept of cognitive flexibility-rigidity as a variable affecting the rater (and the rating) of teaching effectiveness. The principal relevance of the Anderson and Hunka article to the present research, however, has been a point of theoretical reference (Anderson and Hunka, 1963).

In summary, there is in the literature on teacher effectiveness theoretical support for the study of cognitive variables in teaching. With Knoell's exception there appear to be, however, no relevant empirical studies. Significant to the present research is a point made by Getzels and Jackson (1963): "The role played by different types of [cognitive] abilities (divergent thinking) and by attitudinal correlates of ability has yet to be explored. If linked to an adequate conceptualization of teaching, these two types of inquiry may lead us closer to an understanding of how intellectual power contributes to the teacher's behavior and effectiveness in the classroom" (p. 574).

The present investigation has been designed to change the focus of research from attempts to relate static personality or social status variables to an outcome measure such as pupil gain.[1] We have selected a more proximate criterion than pupil learning and a more dynamic set of variables than personality traits or social status indicators. Our approach has been to specify a proximate criterion, teacher competence/effectiveness, in terms of a set of behaviors in the classroom as an important dependent variable.

Concurrently we have attempted to derive and relate these behaviors to a set of concepts which appear specifically pertinent to effective/ineffective teaching, namely cognitive flexibility-rigidity. By this is meant, very simply, the teacher's ability to think on his feet, to adapt teaching objectives, content, and method in process (in response to the reaction, learning difficulties, and needs of the pupils). More broadly, cognitive flexibility refers to dimensions of open-mindedness, adaptability, a resistance to premature perceptual closure.

This research is, thus, oriented toward providing a viable conceptual framework for prediction and evaluation of, in this case, secondary school teaching based on teacher behavior which is observable in the classroom and not dependent on static personal "traits" which cannot be made operational.

Although the research is centered on one variable, we do not imply that cognitive flexibility-rigidity is the single mediating process, the unitary mechanism, or the only relevant variable for effective teaching. In fact, there are most certainly other important dimensions and significant relationships in such a complex set of interactions that occur in the teaching-learning process. As an initial step toward increasing our understanding of effective teaching, however, we have selected this one variable because of its logical relationship both in construct and operation to teacher behavior.

In terms of actual teaching behavior, cognitive flexibility-rigidity necessarily would be inferred largely from the teacher's verbal behavior in interaction with

[1] As surprising as it may be, research has yet to establish that teachers do significantly influence student learning. Research in such a complex area is easily confounded. Thus Howsam suggests: "Since it is not presently feasible to rely on the ultimate criterion of teacher effectiveness, it becomes necessary to attempt to develop intermediate or proximate criteria" (Howsam, 1963, p. 15).

the pupil(s). Nonverbal aspects of this interaction—subtle affective cues such as voice tone or frowning—would be excluded as much as possible since the relationship of cognitive flexibility to such clearly noncognitive variables would be tenuous at best. In this way, limits were placed on the focus for the concept, at least at the operational level.

For the purposes of this research, teaching in an operational sense is approached from three perspectives: the teacher's personal cognitive characteristics (planning), the teacher's cognitive attitude toward the pupil, and the teacher's cognitive attitude toward the communication of subject matter. The three dimensions were created arbitrarily as a means of classifying aspects of flexibility and rigidity which seem logically related. These are the cognitive styles when planning the approach to the pupils and the method of conveying subject content.

The rationale for relating these aspects of teaching to the theoretical concepts of flexibility and rigidity will be developed in the next section along with some operational examples of flexible and rigid behavior within the three categories.

Personal Cognitive Characteristics (Planning Behavior Under Stress)

Planning, especially under stress, represents an important aspect of the first dimension. The flexible-rigid descriptions are as follows:

Flexible	Rigid
Intern shows open-ended lesson planning. Considers alternate ways to communicate content and/or relate to pupils. Can plan for unexpected under stress. Cognitive process appears fluid and unconstrained.	Intern appears dominated by lesson plan, poor plan and use of time, gets trapped in digressions. Cannot handle the unexpected, especially under stress. Cognitive process appears constrained and inhibited.

The intern's ability to plan and modify the plan while teaching was, of course, crucial.[2] At the same time it is necessary to underscore the stressful nature of the classroom situation. The interns found themselves, especially at the outset, unfamiliar with teaching skills, with age and ability differences of secondary school pupils, and with communicating their college major subject in ways understandable to, for example, twelve-fourteen year-olds. Another aspect of the stress was the model of emulation represented by the master teacher, responsible for a rigorous analysis and continuing evaluation of the intern's performance. Stress also derives from an emphasis on self and peer evaluation by interns. In such a

---

2 The research was conducted using a sample of intern teachers. The specifics of the research design are enumerated in the following section—Research Objectives and Procedures.

circumstance the relation between planning and cognitive flexibility-rigidity should be most apparent. Under stress the tendencies toward one or the other extreme should be magnified.

Rokeach (1960) is helpful in understanding the relationship between such stress or anxiety and the operational concepts of flexibility and rigidity:

> If a person feels strongly threatened or anxious in a given situation, he should above all be motivated to act so that the threat is reduced and the anxiety allayed. It is precisely because he is so motivated that the relatively closed person becomes highly attuned to irrelevant internal and external pressures and, accordingly, unable to evaluate information of source (p. 62).

Stress produces, for the person with a closed system, a reliance on irrelevant factors in determining what course of action is to be taken.

Thus, the cognitively rigid person is very likely to act maladaptively. Rokeach (1960) is again helpful in understanding how this stress-anxiety-rigidity system operates. He assumes that there are certain characteristics of a given situation that point to acting appropriately in it. By responding to relevant characteristics, the person's response should be appropriate. Any situation, however, will contain irrelevant factors which, if they determined a person's response, would lead to inappropriate action.

> Every person, then, must be able to evaluate adequately both the relevant and irrelevant information he receives from every situation. This leads us to suggest a basic characteristic that defines the extent to which a person's system is open or closed; namely, the extent to which the person can receive, evaluate, and act on relevant information received from the outside on its own intrinsic merits, unencumbered by irrelevant factors in the situation arising from within the person or from the outside (p. 57).

In the classroom the competing stimuli are numerous. The choice of appropriate teaching content and method (planning) depends on careful assessment of these stimuli. In our view, it is the cognitively flexible teacher who can do this with accuracy, especially when under the stress of classroom teaching.

Cognitive Attitude Toward the Pupil (Responsiveness to the Class)

The amount or level of responsiveness to the class is an important factor in assessing the teacher's cognitive attitude toward the pupil. The flexible-rigid dimension was conceptualized as follows:

Flexible	Rigid
Intern is responsive to the class; sees, listens, and responds to discipline problems, inattention, learning difficulties, students' need for new knowledge and creativity.	Intern doesn't register "cues"; children's problems are tuned out. Calls on bright students too often and doesn't recognize when to call on the slow child.

Previous research seems to indicate that the flexible-rigid dimension is highly relevant to assessing responsiveness to individual differences. Bieri (1955) and Kelly (1955) have found, for example, that people with a more flexible structure as opposed to those with a more rigid structure of constructs are better able to differentiate among objects or situations. Jones (1955), and Scodel and Mussen (1953) both found that authoritarians are more insensitive than nonauthoritarians to the personality characteristics of others and more insensitive to individual differences. These joint findings emphasize the disadvantage at which a cognitively rigid person is placed in attempting to be responsive to individual differences, especially in a class, while implying the obverse for the flexible teacher.

Cognitive Attitude Toward Subject Matter and Teaching Method (Communication)

The use of teaching methods was a central dimension in the assessment of a teacher's cognitive attitude toward the communication of subject matter. The flexible-rigid dimension was conceptualized in the following manner:

Flexible	Rigid
Intern uses a variety of methods, flexibility in implementation of plans, and employs inquiry for effective teaching.	Uses few teaching methods, adheres to one or two formats in planning lessons, and employs a prescriptive rather than problematic teaching approach.

Gardner (1959) has found that subjects classified as constricted / rigid seem particularly resistive to change, "preferring to maintain sets long after they were appropriate, another indication that they could not take advantage of available cues" (p. 53). Translated to the classroom, this would result in the employment of one teaching method until well after its particular contribution has been utilized effectively. The cognitively rigid teacher would miss the cues that another approach was indicated. A constricted perceptual set followed by action in accord with those filtered perceptions would also tend to promote a mechanical presentation of subject matter or a rather prescriptive lecture *at* pupils long after attention and participation by the pupils had waned.

With the above considerations as determinants, a teacher rating scale was developed which linked operational examples to the concepts of flexibility and rigidity. Cognitive rigidity was conceptualized as an inappropriate response keyed to an excessive need for closure, structure, and an intolerance of ambiguity. This would tend to promote a prescriptive rather than problematic style in class identifiable by the limited range of behaviors available to the teacher. At the other end of the hypothetical continuum, cognitive flexibility was viewed as promoting open evaluation and exploration, the disposition to think on one's feet and to consider the value of competing alternative teaching methods rather than accepting a single approach by default.

Research Objectives and Procedures

The objectives of the research were: (1) To derive from the concept of cognitive flexibility operational translations of specific teacher behavior which may serve as a criterion measure, and (2) Within this framework, to investigate the utility of projective instruments as a means to predict teacher performance. The basic assumption was that certain indicators of cognitive flexibility-rigidity derived from the psychological tests would relate consistently to the observed teacher behavior in the classroom.

The sample of 28 subjects (15 male and 13 female) was randomly selected from the population of intern teachers in the Harvard-Newton Summer Program 1964. The subject areas represented were English, Social Studies, Mathematics, and Science.

The program from which our sample was drawn involves one full year of study. The summer segment of the program provides intensive supervised practice teaching for seven weeks. After the summer program, the intern teachers spend half the following academic year as full-time graduate students in residence and serve, under supervision, as paid intern teachers in local school systems for the other half year.

The admission standards to the program are rigorous. The average Graduate Record Examination score for admitted candidates in 1964 was 660 Verbal (94 percentile) and 590 Math (82 percentile). Over half of the accepted applicants in the Master of Arts in Teaching program in 1962 were honor graduates in their major field of study (Sizer, 1962).

Psychological Testing to Predict Flexibility-Rigidity

The psychological tests used as predictors were the Rorschach and the Visual Impressions Tests (VIT), administered before the intern teachers began practice teaching.[3] These tests provided the data for predictions on each dimension of the teacher rating scale.

---

[3] The VIT is a written form of the Thematic Apperception Test using Cards 1, 4, 6 BM, 14, and 7 BM.

The procedures followed in scoring the Rorschach and the VIT were developed for a prior study of elementary school interns (Emlaw, Mosher, Sprinthall, and Whiteley, 1963).

As Zubin (1953) has noted, most studies with the Rorschach which have yielded equivocal results have used the so-called "sign" approach, the use of the Rorschach scoring categories for analysis as discrete variables. This approach was, therefore, not attempted by the writers.

Symonds and Dudek (1956) used the Rorschach in a study of teacher effectiveness to develop a personality description from which predictions are made. With their method, they obtained a rank-order correlation of .60 between Rorschach ratings and teacher effectiveness ratings. A major limitation of the Symonds and Dudek study is that the ratings from the Rorschach were intuitive, as indeed were the ratings of teacher effectiveness. The authors did not provide guidelines for subsequent researchers to follow; thus, their study could not be replicated.

While the Symonds method seems potentially effective, the writers felt that it would be more productive to develop a rating method for using projective tests oriented specifically to the cognitive flexibility dimensions of the teacher rating scale. Rating guidelines were developed so that the scoring procedures can be replicated.

In this study, the Rorschach was used in such a manner as to develop a construct of the subject in the form of, "He seems like the sort of person who _____ ." This method is based on McArthur's (1954) description of the approach of clinicians who were able to make the best predictions about an individual's behavior. Translated to predicting how an individual would teach, the construct would take the form of, "He seems like the sort of person who would teach _____ ." This approach, using the Rorschach data, was applied to each flexible-rigid dimension in the rating scale. A similar approach was employed in analyzing the VIT stories.

Certain aspects of the Rorschach and VIT protocols were of more relevance in considering predictions on specific scales. The weight of each element was determined, however, by its relation to the total test protocols. Table 1 presents the Rorschach and VIT elements associated with the flexible-rigid dimension for cognitive characteristics.

While this subject was able to see the popular figures, he was unable to breathe any life into his perception or to utilize the other aspects of the blot.

The illustrative nature of these examples must be underscored. No single Rorschach response was a major determinant by itself. For example, the intern teacher who gave the flexible response quoted above produced other responses to the balance of the cards which provided a constellation of flexible responses as indicators of personal cognitive flexibility. The obverse is true for the intern who responded in a rigid manner to the same card. Especially at the extremes of the flexibility-rigidity continuum, a remarkable consistency in response patterns appeared which may account for the highly significant relationships between predicted and observed flexibility-rigidity noted later in this report.

TABLE 1

Rorschach Elements Associated with the Flexible-Rigid Dimension for
Personal Cognitive Characteristics

FLEXIBLE	RIGID
R $\geq$ 25	R < 25
F% $\leq$ 50	F% > 50
70 $\leq$ F+% < 90	F+% > 90
W's are W++ and W+	W's are Wm and Wv

FLEXIBLE	RIGID
Vista	No Vista
Content varied	A% > 50, few categories
m < 3	m $\geq$ 3
F(Ch) shading present	Ch shading
FC, CF, M, FM present	FC, CF, FM, M absent or undeveloped

To illustrate scoring for personal cognitive characteristics, the following was considered a flexible response to Card 3.

Performance Proper	Inquiry
It is two natives beating on a drum, with monkeys and a butterfly in the background.	Those things at the top are monkeys hanging from trees, and that is a butterfly in the middle, a red butterfly. It must be a jungle scene.
W+ M,FC,FM H,A,Obj. P	

The subject was able to integrate the disparate parts of the blot into an integral whole response, as well as to utilize a variety of determinants and content. Compare a mediocre response such as:

Performance Proper	Inquiry
Two men with something there in the center.	It looks like a table or something, with the men on both sides.
W F+ H,Obj. P	

Another important dimension of the rating scale for the personal cognitive characteristics variable is the use of humor and other devices to look beyond the immediacy of a situation. The following VIT story to Card 6BM, the older woman and the young man, was told by an intern teacher rated as flexible on this dimension.

So here we have a little old lady who has just been told there is no Santa Claus. This faith in Saint Nick has always been deeply held by her, until the serious young man from the Welcome Wagon crushed it. She is thinking that life is one big deception and if you can't believe in Santa then who can you trust. Well-meaning Joe wishes he'd stuck to being a newspaper boy and realizes he has put his foot in it once again. The little old lady will continue to lose all hope until one day by chance she reads "Christmas Carol." The young man will plod imperceptively through life.

This unusual, highly original story certainly is evidence of an ability to go beyond the immediacy of a presented situation and to employ humor to advantage. The flexible cognitive rating was based in large part on this ability as reflected in the VIT story.

In the following VIT story told to Card 1, the boy with the violin, is an example of a rigid, singularly unimaginative production so characteristic of rigid thinkers.

Johnny was sent into the room to practice the violin. He didn't want to go because everyone was outside playing baseball.

He is now daydreaming about the fun everyone is having outside. He is also pouting over the fact that he has to practice.

Johnny finally picks up the instrument and begins to practice. Eventually this practice proves to be valuable because he ends up as the first violinist in the Champagne Philharmonic under the direction of Lawrence Welk.

The simple plot was left unelaborated. There is no evidence of the capacity to go beyond the immediacy of a situation. Banality is the story's leading characteristic.

The second area in the rating scale concerns the teacher's cognitive attitude toward the pupil. This was assessed from the interaction of the characters in the Rorschach human movement responses and from the interaction of the heroes in the VIT stories. Table 2 summarizes the Rorschach and VIT elements associated with cognitive attitude toward the pupil.

TABLE 2

Rorschach and VIT Elements Associated with the Flexible-Rigid Dimension for Cognitive Attitude Toward the Pupil

FLEXIBLE	RIGID
M interactions are on an equal basis	M interactions condescending
VIT heroes responsive to others	VIT hero "cues" others out
VIT hero sees others as equal human beings	VIT heroes look down on others

The following story was judged rigid:

> Here we have one of those very rare representations of the young Beethoven. The picture is entitled "Young Beethoven Contemplating the Violin of Igor." In case the reader is not familiar with the story, I shall give a brief sketch to outline the legend that accompanies the picture.
>
> Igor, as you may or may not know, was the twelve-year-old friend of Ludwig who lived next door to the composer in Vienna. At the time, Beethoven was several years younger than Igor and had no knowledge of the power of music.
>
> Igor, however, had been taking music lessons for several years and had attained no little proficiency at the violin Unfortunately, the young virtuoso was an insufferable person and a pompous braggard who took every opportunity that presented itself to lord it over Ludwig, ignorant as he was at the time.
>
> The latter, however, was no slouch so to speak, and after listening to the fulminations of Igor for a sufficient amount of time, he decided to compose a violin concerto himself to spite his snooty friend.
>
> This picture then shows the boy Beethoven contemplating what has come to be known as the First Violin Concerto in D. It is most likely scholars are not in total agreement however on this point, that the boy is probably thinking something over, the like of this: "That Igor is nothing short of an absolute boor. Purely for the sake of grinning down my short sleeve shirt at him, I shall compose a concerto on his very own violin. Maybe then all the other kinder on the strasse will believe me when I tell them what a showoff Igor really is."

The story itself was rendered in a condescending manner, as is evident from the remarks such as "in case the reader is not familiar" and "as you may or may not know." The relationship between Igor and Beethoven was used as a major basis for the rigid rating; there was little responsiveness to the other's feelings in the story and the young virtuoso "took every opportunity that presented itself to lord it over Ludwig, ignorant as he was at the time."

The following story told to Card 6BM, the older woman and the young man, was told by an intern teacher rated as having a very flexible cognitive attitude toward the student.

> The son has come to tell his mother that he is engaged to marry a girl he loves very much but who is of another religion. He is troubled because he knows this will hurt his mother, but he has resolved to marry the girl and he tells his mother this. She is not completely surprised, for she has met the girl and has expected such an announcement, but she is still taken aback. She wants to fight this prejudice within her but cannot free herself of it completely. She does like the girl and thinks her a fine girl for her son—and yet . . .
>
> Mother understands son's feelings and gives her "approval."

This story is remarkable for its sensitivity to the feelings of another person: it was this characteristic that in major part determined the flexible rating. The hero in the story was able to respond to a variety of feelings, to anticipate those of the mother, and to assess his own introspectively. It was felt that someone with this capacity for sensitivity as inferred from the VIT would be very responsive to students in the classroom.

The final variable assessed by the rating scale involves the cognitive attitude toward the communication of subject matter. Table 3 presents the Rorschach and VIT elements associated with the flexible-rigid dimension for this variable.

TABLE 3

Rorschach and VIT Elements Associated with the Flexible-Rigid
Dimension for Cognitive Attitude Toward the Communication
of Subject Matter

FLEXIBLE	RIGID
Rorschach is seen as an open-ended task	Rorschach is a given, cut and dried
Capacity for fantasy	No or little fantasy
Will "take a chance" in responding	Reports only the "facts"
Creative use of the blot	Stereotyped reasoning
Flexible sequence	Stereotyped sequence
P present but balanced by O and varied concepts	P over-developed with banal content

As Table 3 indicates, emphasis was placed on the manner in which the responses were communicated to the examiner and how the subject viewed the open-ended Rorschach as a behavioral task.

Consider the following Rorschach response given to Card 4 along with the inquiry, as an example of a rigid cognitive attitude.

Performance Proper	Inquiry
S. That thing in the middle is a slimy worm.	E. What about the blot made it seem like a slimy worm? S. It looks like it. E. Why slimy? S. It is a slimy worm and slimy worms are slimy.

The subject could not dissociate himself enough from the concreteness of his perception to analyze what it was about the inkblot that he used to make his response. The Rorschach was seen as a "given," with what he saw as a response being so "cut and dried" as to be too obvious to require analysis.

A similarly rigid thought process is evident in the following Rorschach response given to Card 10.

Performance Proper	Inquiry
It is a couple of crabs, the blue figures.	E. Where did you see the couple of crabs? S. These blue figures, a number of legs which project out of the body. E. Were your crabs blue? S. Yes, I guess so. E. Are crabs blue? S. I don't know. I think they are red. What part of the country are you from?

Instead of analyzing his answer, the subject attempted to switch the dialogue. The inquiry proved a surprise, as the response hadn't been carefully thought out. The resultant stress was handled, not in terms of the situation, but in terms of the subject's internal reactions.

The following response to Card 10 of the Rorschach was thought to be indicative of a flexible approach.

Performance Proper	Inquiry
It is springtime in Paris, with all the colors.	Of course you have to stretch your imagination a bit, but the Eiffel Tower is at the top and in the center is a pool leading up to the tower and there are flower beds on the side, bright colored flowers.
W+ CF Bot,ld,arch	

In this response, the subject was able to respond with a variety of contents logically elaborated into a meaningful whole response. In addition, the subject was able to "take a chance," to go beyond the obvious characteristics of the situation.

The following response to Card 9 of the Rorschach was likewise considered indicative of flexible thinking.

Performance Proper	Inquiry
Like a scene on a dance floor as seen through a cocktail glass —the figures dancing and the bright costumes they are wearing. W M,FC H,obj,cl O+	It is through a cocktail glass cause the figures aren't distinct. They are seen in rapid motion. The costumes they are wearing seem like Halloween costumes cause they are orange.

This highly imaginative response goes well beyond the obvious stimulus characteristics of the inkblot. The Rorschach was not viewed as a "given" which required answers of precision. While the subject was able to utilize the characteristics of the inkblot, he was not so tied by them that he could not use them to create a varied perception.

An important cognitive characteristic in the flexible communication of subject matter is the ability for creative use of the stimulus or task instead of a stereotyped presentation of just the facts. The following story given to Card 1, the boy with the violin, was told by an intern teacher rated as flexible in the communication of subject matter.

"One more afternoon with this lousy violin and I'll break it over Mr. Planoski's head." Ralph really didn't dislike the music master; in fact, there was a kind of sympathy between them, a sympathy born of mutual ordeal. Ralph knew he would never play the violin, and Mr. Planoski, though he was paid not to admit the distressing fact of his pupil's inability, was equally certain of Ralph's musical ineptness. During the first year of lessons, Ralph played poorly, believing that Mr.

Planoski, discouraged with his pupil's possibilities, would end the hopeless sessions.

But the chain of command was more intricate, Ralph quickly discovered. Whom should he petition? Mother, Sister, Brother, Aunt Mag, Grandfather, Father? There must be someone. There must be some way to convince the household that he and the violin were incompatible.

It was with this very real problem that Ralph wrested on a hot afternoon in August. Break the violin? Break a finger? Buy all the G-strings in the country? No, he had been through all of that before. What he needed was a dramatic effect, a real demonstration that his fortune would not be made in music. But why not a recital? Next weekend when all those people were coming down from the city. He would demand an audience, suggest an after dinner "musicale." And he would implicate as many as possible in the disaster. Aunt Mag would play the piano, Mother the viola, and Father, his viola. Ralph, of course, would have the solo. He chuckled at the possibilities.

This story goes well beyond the "facts" of the picture to which the story was told. The capacity for fantasy, complexity, and elaboration is obvious. It was largely on this basis that the flexible rating was made.

In contrast is the following story told to Card 4, a man and a woman with a pinup in the background, by a subject characterized as quite rigid.

This is a married couple living in a poor house as evidenced by the poster on the wall. It appears that the wife is trying to persuade her husband from doing something—I won't presume to know what—and he is turning away with a rather determined but frustrated look. Thus it remains a question whether or not he listens to his wife and what is probably her plea for social responsibility.

The subject's comment "I won't presume to know what" is indicative of his misconstruing of the task through a narrow conception of it. The directions specified a dramatic story of the subject's creation—yet he interpreted the story as indicative of a "correct" answer. He was unable, again, to respond flexibly to the task and construct an ending to what had been a particularly dull, simple, and unimaginative story. The subject unfortunately was found to teach the way he told stories.

The scoring system which we have outlined above is an attempt to use the Rorschach and TAT in such a manner as to avoid the pitfalls of a completely objective sign approach (for a comprehensive attempt to use the Rorschach in this way see Cooley, 1963). At the same time we have attempted to specify the particular elements of the protocols which we did use in deriving our predictions to avoid a completely intuitive and subjective method. Super notes that the Rorschach does have wide appeal as a research instrument but . . . " At the same time, the enthusiasm of its proponents and the extent to which it has been based on clinical intuition and subjectively rather than quantitatively analyzed experience have antagonized many more scientifically minded psychologists" (Super and Crites, 1963, pp. 560-1).

There are limitations in this scoring system. For example, it was not possible to answer directly the problem of reliability. Nonetheless, in an area of human behavior which has proved until now particularly resistant to significant objective methods of measurement, the Rorschach used in the manner outlined above seems particularly valuable. It provides both an assessment of the important behavioral constellations that are operating and a method for developing significant and substantial predictions.

Procedures for the Teacher Rating Scale

The teacher rating scale was designed to categorize and rate certain cognitive behaviors characteristic of teaching. The categories are broad: (1) The way in which intellectual process is applied in the teaching, (i.e., the cognitive "style" of the teacher); (2) The cognitive attitude adopted toward the pupil; (3) The cognitive attitude characterizing the definition of the teaching objectives, the planning of content, and the teaching method selected. Sub-scales are included under each category. Each sub-scale and the category overall is rated on a five-point cognitive flexibility scale. A score of 1 on any scale would indicate a high adjudged order of cognitive flexibility in teaching; a score of 5, a high adjudged order of cognitive rigidity in teaching. Descriptions of both flexible and rigid teaching behavior are provided for each of the sub-scales.

Two steps were entailed in rating: (1) the selection and specification of several categories of teaching behavior which appeared primarily cognitive in character; and (2) brief descriptions for each sub-scale of (cognitive) teaching behavior that would be regarded as relatively flexible and as relatively rigid. The examples of cognitively flexible and rigid teaching behaviors provided for the guidance of the rater were both modified and amplified as a result. [4]

The ratings were based on a complete period (a 50-60 minute sample) of the intern's teaching. The rater also observed the subject during the supervisory-planning conference which followed the teaching. Neither the subjects nor the supervisory personnel were informed of the rater's purpose.

Ratings of teaching behavior obviously involve an inferential and evaluative process on the part of the rater. As noted in the instrument employed in this study, examples of specific flexible and rigid teaching behaviors are provided for each sub-scale. The purpose was to focus the process of inference and evaluation on certain aspects of teaching behavior hypothesized as indices of the organizing construct.

---

[4] The complete teacher rating scale can be found in the full Office of Education report. Any formal control for interjudge reliability in the use of the instrument was thought to be premature at this stage of the research.

Hopefully, this would serve, too, to reduce intuitive ratings and increase the possibility of replication.[5]

Analysis of Data and Findings

To test the relationship between predicted and observed flexibility-rigidity, three analyses were made: (1) an overall rank order correlation for all intern teachers; (2) a rank order correlation for each of the cognitive sub-scales: (a) Personal characteristics, (b) Attitude toward the pupil, and (c) Attitude toward subject matter; and (3) a chi-square test to examine in particular the efficiency of prediction for the extreme ratings (the top and bottom 25 per cent of the sample).

Overall Rank Order Correlation

The psychological tests provided the basis for the *predicted ratings* along each dimension of the Teacher Rating Scale. The observed ratings of teacher behavior were made during the summer training program. The scores for the sub-scales were totaled for each intern teacher to derive a summary predicted and observed score on the flexibility-rigidity continuum. A rank order was derived on the basis of the predicted and observed scores for each intern. From this a Spearman Rank Correlation Coefficient was computed. The result was an $r=+.53$ between the predicted and observed ranks $(p < .01)$. This indicates a substantial and significant relationship between the predicted and observed scores.

Rank Order Correlations for Each Sub-Scale

The next step was to test the relationship of the observed and predicted scores for each of the three scales. By taking each scale separately, a rank order correlation was computed for the three dimensions. The results are presented in Table 4.

TABLE 4

Rank Order Correlations

(Three Sub-Scales of Cognitive Flexibility-Rigidity)
(Predicted and Observed Ratings N = 28)

Sub-Scale Dimension	Rank Order r
Personal Cognitive Characteristics	+.54 (p < .01)
Cognitive Attitude Toward the Pupil	+.49 (p < .01)
Cognitive Attitude Toward Subject Matter	+.39 (p < .05)

[5] The inclusion of critical incidents or excerpts of teacher-pupil verbal behavior illustrative of cognitive flexibility-rigidity is beyond the scope of the study. Such a scoring guide for raters, however, will be developed in manual form. Attempts to apply the rating scale to typescripts of teacher-pupil dialogue is another potentially useful dimension to be examined. Research along these lines would be a starting point to answer the rater reliability questions.

Table 4 indicates that the correlations of the first two sub-scales, (1) Personal cognitive characteristics and (2) Cognitive attitude toward the pupil, represent the major areas of agreement between the observed and predicted ratings. Our method for rating cognitive attitude toward subject matter was the least indicative of agreement. While the overall findings and the relationship of actual and predicted positions of the first two sub-scales are satisfactory, a revision of method is needed before the third sub-scale system can be considered adequate. The particular aspects of the Rorschach and Visual Impression Test which we hypothesized as relating to cognitive attitude toward subject matter are apparently not sufficiently differentiating without further refinement.

The Chi-Square Test

To examine the efficiency of prediction for each intern, particularly at the extremes of the flexibility-rigidity continuum, we divided the sample into three groups: (1) The seven most flexible (the top quartile, N = 7); (2) the middle group (N = 14); and (3) the seven least flexible (the bottom quartile, N = 7). We compared the predicted and observed rating through a Chi-Square test. The results are presented in Table 5.

TABLE 5

Chi-Square Test

Observed Teacher Performance

		FLEXIBLE	MODERATE	RIGID	
Predicted Teacher Performance	RIGID	0	1	6	7
	MODERATE	2	11	1	14
	FLEXIBLE	5	2	0	7
	N	7	14	7	

$$(x^2 = 25.99, Ndf = 4, sig \leq .001) \qquad \boxed{N = 28}$$

Reading along the diagonal it can be seen that accurate predictions were made for five of seven apprentices rated most flexible. At the other extreme accurate predictions were achieved for six of seven rated most rigid. In no instance was a false positive recorded; a "most flexible" predicted as "most rigid" or vice versa.

These results are encouraging and indicate that the systems for prediction may have relevance to effective and ineffective teaching. The overall correlation was substantial when compared with the results of previous research. Similarly the classification of teachers into extremes of flexibility and rigidity within the sample provides important information for the accuracy of individual predictions.

A Partial Follow-Up of Findings

Although it was not possible within the scope of the research project to replicate the study, some external evidence did support our findings. Subsequent to the
completion of the summer segment of the training program for intern teachers, we
were able to collect partial follow-up information on the research sample interns.
Of the original 28 interns, three were not permitted to continue in the internship
program because of ineffectual teaching performance. These judgements were
made entirely independent of our research findings by the master teacher in conjunction with the particular department chairman in the program. All three of
these candidates were originally rated among the most rigid and predicted as ineffective teachers by our procedures. All other members of the sample were allowed
to continue in the program.

Another indicator of the efficiency of the rating procedure system can be seen
by examining the field reports supplied by the university supervisor—again an
independent judgment of teaching effectiveness. Two of the three remaining interns identified through the research procedures as most rigid have been intern
teachers this fall (the other interns will not teach in school until the second term).
Excerpts on these two interns supply some cross-validation to our findings. One
supervisor wrote after one month of observation:

"The intern has yet to do any effective teaching . . . the lessons have no sense of
purpose . . . there is very limited participation by the pupils—few questions. Generally the intern lectures *at* the class and seems literally oblivious of the children
shifting restlessly in their seats—doodling. I have serious reservations concerning
this intern's competence and request additional supervisory judgment." *

A university supervisor wrote concerning the second intern:

"There is no question that this intern has all kinds of potential, that is, intellectual and subject matter, but he doesn't *see* the pupils, he doesn't *hear* them . . .
They're just not in his focus."

At the other extreme, two of the interns predicted most flexible have also been
teaching this semester (again, the others rated most flexible will not be in the
schools until the second semester). The field supervisor for one intern reports:

"The intern uses varied materials and techniques with facility . . . concentrates
on listening to pupils . . . Overall the intern's performance in the classroom is
superior, in fact better than some experienced teachers in this system."

The second intern was described as follows:

"Already a 'master' teacher, I would never guess that the intern was a beginner,
the classes are so well taught—well-planned yet spontaneous. The intern skillfully

---

* This report and the others quoted were filed with the internship program as part of their regular evaluation procedures and were not written especially for the research project. In fact, neither the
schools, the school supervisors, nor the regular supervisory members of the university staff had any
knowledge as to which interns we had selected from the population for the project.

changes problems, presents many different ways of approach to problems, is full of questions for the class, and still exhibits marvelous control . . . " /

To recapitulate, using the psychological tests, we were able to predict accurately six of seven interns rated most rigid by the research associate using the Teacher Rating Scale. Subsequent to the completion of the research project, three of these six trainees were dropped from the internship program because of ineffective teaching performance. Present field reports of two of the remaining interns predicted most rigid indicate continuing ineffectual behavior in the classroom. Thus, for five of the interns originally predicted most rigid, follow-up data strongly supports the predictions. The accuracy of the procedures was also supported for the interns predicted most flexible. Although data was available for only two of the interns, the field reports confirm their effectiveness in teaching performance.

Conclusions and Implications

The research findings indicate support for the basic hypothesis that effective teaching is related to cognitive flexibility. The overall findings were: (1) The dimension of cognitive flexibility-rigidity may represent a critical and differentiating factor in teaching. (2) The research method for prediction along this dimension was found accurate using particular aspects of the Rorschach and TAT administered prior to entry into the teacher training program. (3) The method for prediction of teacher behavior for the first two sub-scales of cognitive flexibility-rigidity, (a) Personal cognitive characteristics or cognitive "style" and (b) Cognitive attitude toward the pupils, was most significantly related to observed performance. (4) Partial follow-up data indicate some cross-validation for the predictions of effective and ineffective teacher behavior, particularly for the most flexible and most rigid groups (the top and bottom quartiles of the sample). (5) Finally, the results from the present study are highly congruent with an earlier study using elementary school intern teachers.

Perhaps a most serious implication from this study was the lack of behavior change within the group of apprentice teachers identified as most rigid and hence predicted to be most ineffective in the classroom. All of these students received intensive supervision by highly skilled master teachers during the summer program yet showed little capacity to upset our predictions. Three of the seven predicted as most rigid were dropped from the program at the end of the summer. The two who have continued as intern teachers this semester have received pessimistic evaluations, again in spite of further efforts under supervision to promote more effective performance.

There may be a need to develop special supervision and training techniques which go beyond the usual procedures presently available before any firm conclusions can be drawn. It may be crucial to examine under what circumstances a change is possible and under what circumstances alternative careers to teaching should be considered. It is apparent that under the present system the cognitively rigid student teacher is unable to modify his behavior significantly.

It is obvious, due to the relatively small sample size and the pilot nature of this project, that additional work is needed. Specifically: (1) Refinements are necessary in the prediction methods. The Rorschach and TAT indicators for cognitive attitude toward the communication of subject matter are not as directly relevant to observed performance as are the first two flexibility-rigidity scales. (2) The Teacher Behavior Rating Scale also ought to be subject to further research. It is necessary to draw up a training manual as a guide for use by teacher-supervisors. Then the problem of evaluation and reliability could be directly studied. (3) Further evidence is definitely needed to establish the degree to which a cognitively rigid apprentice teacher can change from ineffective to effective behavior in the classroom. At a time when selective admission procedures are becoming possible in teacher training, this has practical implications. Even more important, however, may be the conceptual implication of the stability for cognitive rigidity and flexibility as personality parameters.

While the above limitations are explicit, the research investigation does suggest that the organizing construct, the predictive system, and the rating procedure are consistent and linked to a generic and recognizable conception of teaching.

BIBLIOGRAPHY

Allport, G. *Pattern and Growth in Personality*. New York: Holt, Rinehart and Winston, 1961.

Anderson, C. C., and S. M. Hunka. "Teacher evaluation: Some problems and a proposal," *Harvard Educational Review, 33*, Winter, 1963, 74-93.

Biddle, Bruce J. "The integration of teacher effectiveness research," in Bruce J. Biddle and William J. Ellena (eds.). *Contemporary Research on Teacher Effectiveness*. New York: Holt, Rinehart and Winston, 1964, 1-40.

Bieri, J. "Cognitive Complexity-Simplicity and Predictive Behavior," *Journal of Abnormal and Social Psychology, 51*, 1955, 263-68.

Cooley, William W. *Career Development of Scientists*. Cooperative Research Project No. 436. Washington, D. C.: U. S. Department of Health, Education and Welfare, 1963.

Domas, S. J., and D. V. Tiedeman. "Teacher competence: An annotated bibliography," *Journal of Experimental Education, 19*, December, 1950, 99-218.

Emlaw, R., R. Mosher, N. Sprinthall, and J. Whiteley. "Teacher effectiveness: A method for prediction and evaluation," *National Elementary Principal, 43*, 1963, 38-49.

Fattu, Nicholas A. "Research on teacher evaluation," *National Elementary Principal, 43*, 1963, 19-27.

Frenkel-Brunswik, Else. "Patterns of social and cognitive outlook in children and parents," *American Journal of Orthopsychiatry, 21*, 1951, 543-558.

Gardner, R., *et al.* "Cognitive control: A study of individual consistencies in cognitive behavior," *Psychological Issues* I, *4.* New York: International Universities Press, 1959.

Getzels, J. W., and P. W. Jackson. "The teacher's personality and characteristics," in N. L. Gage (ed.). *Handbook of Research on Teaching.* Chicago: Rand McNally and Company, 1964, 506-582.

Goodlad, John I. "The teacher selects, plans, organizes," *Learning and the Teacher,* 1959 Yearbook of the Association for Supervision and Curriculum Development. Washington, D. C.: National Education Association.

Guilford, J. P. *Personality.* New York: McGraw-Hill, 1959.

Howsam, Robert B. "Teacher evaluation: Facts and folklore," *National Elementary Principal, 43*, 1963, 7-18.

Jones E. E. "Authoritatianism as a determinant of first-impression formation," *Journal of Personality, 23*, 1955, 107-127.

Kelly, G. *The Psychology of Personal Constructs.* New York: Norton, 1955.

Knoell, D. M. "Prediction of teaching success from world fluency data," *Journal of Educational Research, 46*, 1953, 673-683.

McArthur, C. "Analyzing the clinical process," *Journal of Counseling Psychology, 4*, 1954, 203-206.

Morsh, J. E. and E. W. Wilder. "Identifying the effective instructor: A review of the quantitative studies 1900-1952." *USAF Personnel Training Research Center (Research Bulletin)* (No. AFPTRC-TR-54-44, 1954.

Rokeach, M. "The nature and meaning of dogmatism," *Psychological Review, 64*, 1954, 194-204.

Rokeach, M. *The Open and Closed Mind.* New York: Basic Books, 1960.

Ryans, D. G. *Characteristics of Teachers.* Washington D. C.: American Council on Education, 1960.

Scodel, A., and P. Mussen. "Social perceptions of authoritarians and nonauthoritarians," *Journal of Abnormal and Social Psychology, 48*, 1953, 181-184.

Shaffer, J., S. Mednick, and Judith Seder. "Some developmental factors related to field-independence in children." *American Psychologist, 12*, 1957.

Sizer, Theodore R. "Master of arts in teaching, Harvard's first 25 years, 1936-1961," A Report to the Administrative Board, Master of Arts in Teaching Program, Cambridge: Harvard College, 1962.

Super, D. E., and J. O. Crites. *Appraising Vocational Fitness.* New York: Harper and Row, 1962.

Symonds, P., and S. Dudek. "Use of the Rorschach in the diagnosis of teacher effectiveness," *Journal of Projective Techniques, 20*, 1956, 227-234.

Witkin, H., *et al. Personality Through Perception.* New York: Harper and Brothers, 1954.

Zubin, J. "Failures of the Rorschach technique," *Journal of Projective Techniques, 18*, 1954, 303-315.

3

Dimensions of Counselor Behavior Related to Cognitive Flexibility Theory

The translation of cognitive flexibility-rigidity into operational, behavioral terms presents a crucial research problem. In Chapter 2, such an operational translation was made in the field of teaching, with an emphasis on observable teacher behavior in the classroom.

In this chapter, a parallel translation will be made of flexibility theory into dimensions of counselor behavior. This provides a sharp break from using overall "global" judgments where a group of counselor educators, after observing counselor candidates, rank orders them on some unspecified criteria. The major shortcoming of this approach is simply that bases for judgment are almost entirely intuitive (for example, see Blocher, 1963). No indication is given as to what kind of behavior distinguished those subjects adjudged most competent from those considered least competent. It is necessary, in terms of possible replication, to have some explicit guidelines which indicate how students were rated. This also obviously requires rather explicit theoretical statements from which operational judgments may be derived.

Cognitive flexibility theory has the capacity for providing explicit guidelines for evaluating counselor behavior. Before proceeding with the translation into operational terms, however, it is first necessary to survey several definitions of counseling as a background to relating flexibility to counseling and counselor effectiveness.

The Definition Problem in Counseling

The number of definitions of counseling is almost infinite. Rather than attempt any systematic review of the literature, we have selected certain contributions that are particularly relevant. The conceptions of Perry, Bordin, Hummel, and Tyler in specific reference to counseling psychology are pertinent. These authors in varying degrees stress the importance of both emotions and rationality in the context of their counseling models. It is on this recognition of the importance of both feelings and ideas that a definition of counseling theory and practice may be effectively based.

Perry (1955) identifies two dimensions of counseling: (a) the "direction of regard" by client and counselor, and (b) the intensity of involvement. In counseling, the counselor and client often examine the latter's role areas or role problems. The term "role" refers to various sectors or areas of the counselee's present social existence. In an educational setting, for example, the individual's major role is as a student confronted with certain educational and vocational decisions. For Perry, counseling would focus on the social roles with which the individual is concerned. Counseling is not directed toward broader aspects of personality, or "psychodynamics," the interplay of instinctual and unconscious forces affecting human behavior.

The intensity of the counseling involvement represents a second parameter. The counselor in the Perry model works with the client on the pertinent role area problems. Therefore, the intensity of the counseling relationship will be significantly different from that typical of psychotherapy. Transference will be at a minimum. Perry also notes that the so-called "personal" or "psychological" counseling would still fit the role problem framework .

> This position can be defended on two grounds (1) In one set of conditions the word "personal" turns out to mean "social"; the person comes to the counselor about his personality in a social sense . . . or (2) he comes, in a general dissatisfaction in his function in most of his roles . . . (Perry, 1955, 404).

Counseling, then, connotes the role problem solving. The client can be aided in learning "the skills of choice and management among life's role" (Perry, 1955, p. 401).

Bordin's (1955) work is relevant because he also emphasizes a counseling model directed toward a problem solving process. Counseling is focused on the rational elements in this process rather than on the intensely affective areas. This does not deny the reality of emotional and irrational forces. Bordin suggests a cognitive-conative balance through which the counselor, while acknowledging the latter, works toward enhancing the former. The array of personality variables involved in any such dimension is, of course, infinite. However, Bordin takes particular note of that segment of personality which is mostly involved with the organization of plans, choice among alternate plans, and what is sometimes called purposive action.

The differentiation between the cognitive and conative is similar to the distinction in psychoanalytic terms between the ego and id. In a sense, Bordin is revising the more traditional analytic theory of personality to include a greater emphasis on ego functions of thought, planning, and problem solving. This framework of ego processes then becomes an acknowledged basis for a viable counseling theory.

Hummel's (1963) work in developing an ego-counseling model represents another important theoretical contribution to a general definition for counseling. A central distinguishing feature of Hummel's "ego-counseling" is the importance it ascribes, theoretically and methodologically, to "secondary process" (to the ego functions of impulse control, planning, logical thinking, and problem solving). Ego-counseling is operationally involved with cognition—with analysis and thinking activity. The particular focus is on the *personal condition* of the individual, reasoning about and revising one's own (rather than abstract or others') reality, problems, plans, and actions. A concern with cognitive theory follows logically. In short, the special "cognitive-conative balance" characterizing ego-counseling derives support both from ego theory (from Allport, Hartman, Bronfenbrenner) and from the "fruitful promise for counseling theorists in the work of Piaget, Bruner, Rapaport, George Kelly, and of others who have inquired into the nature of thinking" (Hummel, 1963, p. 469).

Ego-counseling is not a narrow or naive (pre-Freudian) rationalism. It assumes, however, that ego energy and ego processes can be functionally autonomous within the personality structure; that, in Allport's terms, "the rational functioning of the proprium (ego) is capable . . . of yielding true solutions, appropriate adjustments, accurate planning, and a relatively faultless solving of the equations of life" (Allport, 1961, p. 46).

Tyler's (1964) recent outline of counseling clearly relates to these notions. She construes counseling as the "appraisal with" the client of the array of alternative "possibility structures." The goal is an enhanced rational understanding by a client to enable him to choose the most appropriate course of action. Although Tyler's terminology is somewhat distinct because of her orientation toward individual differences as the basis for theory, there is an analogue between her concept of appraisal and the concept of counseling advanced by the contributors already noted. Her term "possibility structure" refers to the long range strategies for choosing that are possible for an individual. Other theorists identify this concept as ego organization (Hummel), or ego processes (Bordin). Further extensions of counseling theory may be derived from this aspect of personality.

The framework we have sketched is related to some of the prescriptive statements about counseling made over the past ten years. For example, the Northwestern Conference (1951) called for the goals of "fostering psychological development" and emphasizing "the positive and the preventative." In 1956, the Commission on Definition of APA used the phrase "to develop personal resources for the individual" as the emphasis for counseling. Brayfield (1964) denotes human effectiveness as the appropriate counseling orientation. Along these lines Tiedeman (1961) suggests the goal of primary rather than secondary prevention of mental illness as the framework for counseling. Super's (1955) contributions also are relevant, particularly his assertation for a counseling base in "hygiology," the locating and developing of personal and social resources and adaptive tendencies within the individual. Such statements indicate a common core for counseling theory and perhaps even a common methodology, as Samler suggests (1964). The difficulty with such statements, however, is that the consensus looks so real that further theoretical and empirical efforts cease. We have pointed to the lack of solid

research as well as the danger that the social need for counseling becomes the definition of counseling.

The counselor's role and function can be viewed within the basically cognitive
model derived from the literature. For example, the counselor provides special
individual assistance to relatively normal clients. As Tyler notes, the client does not
necessarily need to have a "presenting problem" since the aim is for increased
effectiveness of choice behavior. However, the nature of our present society confronts the individual with certain discontinuities and therefore requires choice.
This is particularly true for the period of adolescent development. In settings such
as school or college, the student population is confronted with the realities of
choice; educational, vocational, and personal decisions must be made. At any
given point, some of these students may not resolve these role area concerns. The
complexity inherent in our increasingly technological corporate and bureaucratic
structures means that decisions become categorical imperatives with attendent
"real" anxieties. "No longer can youth contemplate its future under the protection
of the great social stabilizers of the past. No longer can one counsel within the
framework of Victorian decorum, theological certainties, or the Pax Britannica"
(Allport, 1962, p. 377). The simple time lag of prolonged adolescence that our
educational system imposes serves to heighten the problem of adequate decision
making and performance by our youth. The extensive "rites of passage" before
assuming positions of responsibility create the ground upon which the counselor
and client stand.

The concerns noted above, while creating a need or the opportunity for service,
also indicate an appropriate framework for the remedy. The goal of counseling as
we have defined it involves the channeling of cognitive abilities for effective self
management. This may lead to the generalities of human effectiveness, ego
strength, and autonomy, enhanced through process. We hope to derive from this
framework operations more explicit to the area of cognition and problem solving.

Operational Definitions of Cognitive Flexibility in Counseling

Cognitive flexibility represents for the writers a most relevant dimension in effective counseling behavior, particularly in the areas of cognition and problem
solving. Effective counselor behavior results from the ability to remain cognitively
flexible; to respond, for example, to both the content and feeling which the client
communicates. The implication is that the rigid counselor, unable to respond to
the demands of the interaction with the client, construes the situation in terms of
his own frame of reference. This might take the form of seeking early closure on
the client's problems and systematically "tuning out" additional responses by
the client.

In specific reference to counseling, Van Kaam (1962) discussed rigid behavior
in his presentation of creativity as an attitude of the mature counselor. He sees
rigid behavior as a "defense against the possible challenge of an unexpected world,

a world which is communicated to us and which may expose us to our own repressed regions of being" (p. 408). The mature counselor "can be serious, gay, or detached according to the challenge of the situation. He adopts none of these attitudes compulsively; his behavior is not identical in different situations." The central idea is that the counselor's repertoire of behavior is varied according to the dictates of the situation, not according to his own compulsive structuring. The concept of flexibility-rigidity is seen as the determinant influence on the counselor's ability to respond to the varied modes through which the client presents himself.

Our assumption is that an individual can "know" as well as "experience," that effective counseling need not be encapsulated by some nonrational, completely subjective mystique of "reflected feelings." The dichotomy of content versus feelings as a choice point for counselor response is artificial in our view. We wish to emphasize the importance of both sides of the human condition of ideas and emotions. The flexible counselor can respond to both content and feelings—he can answer questions and keep open the exploration by the client; he can avoid either excessive structuring (advice and direction) or the complete ambiguity of nondirection. The counselor is not straight-jacketed by any particular orthodoxy. The concept by its nature implies a less orthodox, less arbitrary position regarding all the common enumerations of so-called counseling methods or techniques.

Significantly, research by Seeman (1948), Snyder (1945), and McGowan, (1954 and 1962) on counseling style indicates that counselors in general follow either the content or the feeling mode in responding to clients. Our point is that it is not necessarily appropriate to rely predominantly on either mode. The authors are fully aware of the general idea, noted by McGowan (1962), that a counseling style which seems to respond to cognition is often equated with "bad" counseling. After all the tremendous effort which counselor education programs have exerted to teach apprentice counselors to respond exclusively in one mode, this should come as no surprise. It is perhaps surprising, as well as ironic, that the nondirective concepts which Rogers originally applied to counseling have more recently become the basis for psychotherapy. The original counseling dimension has been dropped.[1] The function is now more closely identified as long-term psychotherapy, not counseling. There is, however, a strong residue created by the total acceptance of the original nondirective concepts as appropriate to counseling, an acceptance which hinders flexibility, openness and, effective communication.[2]

---

1 Perry (1955) documents the change from counseling to psychotherapy in the Rogerian school over the past 12-15 years. He notes that the recent focus is more on psychodynamics, from short-term cases to cases involving many sessions. He even notes that the references to the term "counseling" declined astonishingly from over 200 in the 1942 volume to a single reference by 1954.

2 In the process of counselor training, we have been particularly struck by the amount of guilt an apprentice counselor experiences when he responds to the content of what the client says, even if it's but once in an hour! We view this as an unfortunate by-product of the dictum to be completely subjective in the counseling process where the counselor is warned against any of his "objective" thoughts.

A Rating Scheme of Counselor Behavior

The counseling process is an extraordinarily complex interpersonal interaction which cannot be reduced to a rating scheme without dangers of oversimplification. The writers propose, however, that suitable operational translations of important dimensions in the counseling process can be derived which fit the concept of cognitive flexibility-rigidity.

Most counseling theorists imply that one of the major dimensions in the counseling process comprehends the examination and exploration by the client of his present concerns. Examples are Tyler's concept of appraisal with the client, Perry's phrase the "heuristic set" of client and counselor, Bordin's "mutual deliberation," and Hummel's "analysis." Clearly, then, this is one dimension of significance in the counseling process—the examination and exploration of the client's problems. Derived from the theoretical framework of flexibility-rigidity, we propose the following scheme as a method of rating scales at the operational level. The counselor's responses are judged according to explicit examples of rigid or flexible behavior within the context of client exploration. For example, in a counseling interview, a client may present a "problem" or a personal concern. The counselor's response or set of responses will enhance or restrict the examination and exploration depending, we hypothesize, on the degree of his flexibility or rigidity.

The counselor in this model is not expected to respond in a single orthodox manner as he meets and works with the client. From the open exploration of the client's present position, the expectation is that the client's awareness and insight will be increased. It is in this context that we lodge the relationship dimension, so important and generic to all counseling theories. Thus, rather than attempt to create a system to rate the quality of the counseling relationship in terms such as "accurate empathy" or tones such as "warm and accepting," we view the relationship in the context of the counselor-client exploration.

The act of professional concern by the counselor in responding in a manner which focuses on the client's perceptions and feelings, and which provides for an open-ended examination of these concerns without recourse to authoritative judgments, represents the relationship in the context of the purposes of counseling. In a sense, the "relationship" in the abstract is derivative from the counselor's focus on the client's concerns, and his flexibility in response to those concerns.

It is necessary to point out that we have based these conceptions on the assumptions of a population of relatively normal students in an educational setting. With severe problems of an emotional nature, the relationship intrinsically assumes a greater significance. We find Perry's notion of the relationship in the context of a "sensed triangle": counselor, client, role problem, as appropriate to counseling. In the more severe instances, the orthodox position would hold, emphasizing the crucial importance of complete empathy and/or transference. Typically, the client has the ability to move rather quickly into the kind of open exam-

ination of the "problem" we describe, if the counselor is flexible enough to encourage this kind of collaboration.

The scale for rating cognitive flexibility as a dimension of counselor behavior
has three broad categories: (1) an overall rating of the way in which intellectual
process is applied in counseling; (2) the degree of exploration and examination in
the client-counselor interaction; and (3) the cognitive attitude adopted toward the
supervision process. Sub-scales are included under each category.

The broad categories, sub-scales, and behavioral descriptions of cognitive flexibility-rigidity in counseling were derived primarily from the writers' experience
table in the supervision of student counselors. Two basic steps were involved in
the development of the rating scale in its current form. The first involved the
selection and specification of several categories of counseling behavior having
some construct validity as primarily cognitive in character. The second step consisted of the construction of brief descriptions for each sub-scale of counseling
behavior that could be regarded as relatively flexible and relatively rigid. Each
sub-scale and summary category was rated on a seven point scale, with a score
of 1 on any scale indicating a high adjudged order of cognitive flexibility in
counseling; a score of 7, a high adjudged order of cognitive ridigity in counseling.

An initial version of the rating scale was discussed with the six Harvard faculty supervisors for 1964-65. The examples of cognitively flexible and rigid counseling behaviors provided for the guidance of the rater were both modified and
amplified as a result.

The first broad category reflected the overall competence in counseling as inferred from cognitive dimensions. The range is from extremely effective to negative effectiveness.

RATING SCALE DIMENSIONS

Flexible					Rigid	
1	2	3	4	5	6	7
Extremely effec-tive; works well with clients; ap-proaches "ideal."		Average com-petence; some shortcomings but generally responsive to clients.		Minimal effec-tiveness. Goes through the motions.		Negative effec-tiveness. Does not really listen or understand clients. Preoccu-pied with himself or irrelevancies.

The second broad category centers on exploration and examination. Within the
client-counselor interation, the focus is on the client's perspective, the effective
repertoire of counselor responses, the amount and quality of interpretation, the
ability to handle the unexpected, and professional objectivity.

RATING SCALE DIMENSIONS

Flexible				Rigid		
1	2	3	4	5	6	7

A. Counselor effectively collaborates with clients—explores and examines *with*.

Early closure on presenting problem—little exploration *with* client.

1	2	3	4	5	6	7

B. Focus on client's perspective.

Gathering information for its own sake.

1	2	3	4	5	6	7

C. Flexible responses. Effective repertoires—to feelings, content, and comment on process when appropriate.

Rigid set of responses. Counselor appears straight-jacketed in one mode.

1	2	3	4	5	6	7

D. Professionally objective — works within limits of role as counselor.

Overinvolvement with clients (rescue or adoption fantasies) or excessive distance to client —appears reserved—"wooden."

1	2	3	4	5	6	7

E. Can handle the unexpected, situational contingencies such as outside interruptions or sudden shifts in affect, mood, discussion.

Gets confused in unexpected situations. Seems trapped, appears not to know what to do —flounders.

1	2	3	4	5	6	7

F. Interpretation or the suggestion of alternative perceptions, if used, remains close to client's level of awareness— offered tentatively to engage the client's participation and consideration.

Interpretation appears as an exercise of the counselor's intellectual prowess—attempts to "thread the needle" with extended discussions.

The third broad category centers on supervision, with particular attention to whether the counselor is open to alternatives and whether he understands the dynamic complexities in counseling.

RATING SCALE DIMENSIONS

	Flexible				Rigid	
1	2	3	4	5	6	7

A. Listens openly to supervisor. Picks up cues from own tapes. Develops an effective but personally idiosyncratic style.

Appears not to hear supervisor—screens out cues—defends doggedly initial positions. Tries to imitate other styles.

1	2	3	4	5	6	7

B. Accurately understands the dynamic complexities of the psychological process within clients, *i.e.*, "normal" problems developmental stages—abnormal, long standing, disruptive problems. Can convey to supervisor awareness of areas of strength as well as weakness.

Either naive grasp of dynamics or overintellectual (bookish) labeling of categories. Conveys to supervisor the impression that counseling is either "magic" or the classification of clients by "types" or "labels."

1	2	3	4	5	6	7

C. Consults appropriately with school personnel (teachers and administrators).

Provides too much information (gossip) or too little (hides under the cloak of confidentiality to school).

1	2	3	4	5	6	7

D. Has a professional commitment to counseling as a career emerges. Collaborates well with supervisor. Uses supervision to focus on "self" in role of counselor.

Little committment or personal involvement in counseling as career—often discusses irrelevant issues in supervision; seems to "miss" appointments; some signs of genuine disinterest; excessive complaints on minor issues of "pollyannaish."

Rating of counseling behavior obviously involves an inferential and evaluative process by the supervisor. As previously noted, the counselor rating scale used in this study provides examples of specific flexible and rigid counseling behaviors for each sub-scale. The purpose is to focus the rating process on counseling behaviors hypothesized as indices of the organizing flexibility-rigidity construct. This serves, hopefully, to reduce intuitive ratings and increase the possibility of replication studies.

A central idea behind the counselor rating scale is that the counselor's repertoire of behavior is varied according to the dictates of the client's situation, not according to the counselor's preconceived structuring of the case.

Counseling aims at the general goal of enhanced rational awareness rather than providing for a specific solution to a particular problem. Through examination and exploration, the client learns a way of approaching problems, perceiving options, and acting more effectively. Counseling in this framework is concerned with both the thoughts and feelings of the clients.

The counselor himself is obviously an important dimension in the counseling process. The traditional area of research has involved studies of counselor characteristics or traits. The assumptions of this approach are at least problematic and certainly the research evidence is equivocal. While human qualities may indeed be relevant to counseling, particular counselor behaviors are a more relevant criterion of counselor effectiveness.

Cognitive flexibility appears as a critical concept in regard to counselor competence. We hold that effective counselor behavior results from the ability to remain cognitively flexible, to promote an open and searching examination of many perceptual and action possibilities.

The concept of flexibility-rigidity is seen as the determining influence on the counselor's ability to respond to the varied modes through which the client presents himself.

Derived from the theoretical framework of flexibility-rigidity, we have proposed a tentative scheme where the counselor's responses are judged according to explicit examples of rigid or flexible behavior within the context of client exploration. This illustrates a major implication of this chapter; namely, that the counseling process be studied from a perspective different from the traditional directive, non-directive controversy. The present orthodoxies surrounding the counselor as teacher or as a reflective "mirror" reify and obfuscate the development of a professional role. New definitions and a research focus on counselor behavior indicate a direction. In order to achieve goals of independent and responsible action by the client, the counselor's own freedom and flexibility are necessary, if ironic, analogues!

BIBLIOGRAPHY

Adrain, E. "The physiological basis of perception." in F. Delafresnaye (ed.). *Brain Mechanisms and Consciousness.* Oxford: Blackwell, 1954, 237-43.

Adorno, T. *et al. The Authoritarian Personality.* New York: Harper, 1950.

Allport, G. W. *Pattern and Growth in Personality.* New York: Holt, Rinehart and Winston, 1961.

Allport, G. W. "Psychological models for guidance," *Harvard Educational Review, 32,* 1962, 373-381.

American Psychological Association, Division of Counseling Psychology, Sub-Committee on Counselor Selection and Counselor Training. *Journal of Counseling Psychology, 1,* 1954, 174-179.

American School Counselor Association. "Proposed statement of policy for secondary school counselors," *ASCA Counselor Study,* February, 1964.

Anderson, C. and S. Hunka. "Teacher evaluation: Some problems and a proposal," *Harvard Educational Review, 33,* 1963, 74-95.

Barron, F. "Originality in relation to personality and intellect," *Journal of Personality, 25,* 1956, 730-42.

Bieri, J. "Cognitive complexity-simplicity and predictive behavior," *Journal of Abnormal Social Psychology, 51,* 1955, 263-68.

Blocher, D. H. "A multiple regression approach to predicting success in a counselor education program." *Counselor Education and Supervision, 3,* 1963, 19-22.

Bordin, E. S. *Psychological Counseling.* New York: Appleton-Century-Crofts, 1955.

Brayfield, A. H. "Counseling," *Annual Review of Psychology, 14,* 1963, 319-350.

Brayfield, A. H. "Counseling psychology." Speech delivered at Greyston Conference on Professional Preparation in Counseling Psychology, Jan. 23, 1964 (mimeo).

Bruner, J. "On perceptual readiness," *Psychological Review, 64,* 1957, 123-152.

Conant, J. B. *The American High School Today.* New York: McGraw-Hill, 1959.

Cottle, W. C. "Personal characteristics of counselors," *Personnel and Guidance Journal, 31,* 1953, 445-450.

Cox, R. D. *Counselors and Their Work.* Harrisburg: Archives Press, 1945.

Cremin, L. A. "The progressive heritage of the guidance movement," *Harvard Educational Bulletin, 8,* 1964, 1-5.

Farson, R. E. "The counselor is a woman," *Journal of Counseling Psychology, 1,* 1954, 221-23.

Fiedler, F. "The concept of an ideal therapeutic relationship," *Journal of Counseling Psychology, 14,* 1950, 239-45.

Gardner, R. *et al. Cognitive Control.* New York: International Universities Press, 1959.

Hill, G. E. "The selection of school counselors," *Personnel and Guidance Journal, 39,* 1961, 355-360.

Hollbrook, D. "The teacher's right to write," *The Spectator, 6973,* Feb. 16, 1962, 201-02.

Howsam, R. B. "Teacher evaluation: Facts and folklore," *National Elementary School Principal, 43,* 1963, 6-18.

Hummel, R. C. "Ego-counseling in guidance: Concept and method," *Harvard Educational Review, 32*, 1962, 463-482.

Klein, G. "Cognitive control and motivation," in G. Lindsey (ed.). *Assessment of Human Motives.* New York: Rinehart, 1958, 87-118.

Kogan, N. and M. Wallach, "Certainty of judgment and evaluation of risk," *Psychological Reports, 6*, 207-13.

Maslow, A., and B. Mittelman. *Principles of Abnormal Psychology.* New York: Harper, 1951.

McGowan, J. "Client anticipations and expectancies as related to initial interview performance and perception." Unpublished Ed. D. Dissertation, University of Missouri, 1954.

McGowan, J. "Developing a natural counseling style," in J. McGowan and L. Schmidt. *Counseling: Readings in Theory and Practice.* New York: Holt, 1962, 368-71.

Patterson, C. H. "The NDEA and counselor education," *Counselor Education and Supervision, 3*, 1963, 4-7.

Perry, W. G. "On the relation of psychotherapy and counseling," *Annals of New York Academy of Sciences, 63*, Nov., 1955, 396-407.

Rogers, C. *Counseling and Psychotherapy.* New York: Houghton Mifflin, 1942.

Rogers, C. R. *Client-Centered Therapy.* New York: Houghton Mifflin, 1957.

Rogers, C. R. "The interpersonal relationship: The core of guidance," *Harvard Educational Review, 32*, 1962, 416-429.

Rokeach, M. *The Open and Closed Mind.* New York: Basic Books, 1960.

Samler, J. "Where do counseling psychologists work?" Speech presented at Greystone Conference, Jan. 23, 1964 (mimeo).

Sanford, N. "The approach of the authoritarian personality," in J. McCary (ed.). *Psychology of Personality.* New York: Grove Press, 1956, 201-52.

Seeman, J. "A study of preliminary interview methods in vocational counseling and client reactions to counseling." Unpublished Doctoral Dissertation, University of Minnesota, 1948.

Shoben, E. J., Jr. "Guidance: Remedial function or social reconstruction," *Harvard Educational Review, 32*, 1962, 430-443.

Snyder, W. "An investigation of the nature of non-directive psychotherapy," *Journal of Genetic Psychology, 33*, 1945, 193-224.

Sprinthall, N. A., J. M. Whiteley, and R. L. Mosher, "Prediction and evaluation of teacher effectiveness at the secondary school level." Cooperative Research Project S-143, U.S. Dept. of Health, Education and Welfare. Washington, D. C.

Super, D. E. "Transition: From vocational guidance to counseling psychology," *Journal of Counseling Psychology, 2*, 1955, 3-9.

Tiedeman, D. V. Appendix 5 in *Action for Mental Health*, final report. New York: Basic Books, 1961, 318-320.

Tiedeman, D. V., and F. L. Field. "Guidance: The science of purposeful action applied through education," *Harvard Educational Review, 32*, 1962, 483-501.

Tyler, L. "The methods and processes of appraisal and counseling." Speech delivered at Greystone Conference, Jan. 24, 1964 (mimeo).

Van Kaam, A. "Counseling from the viewpoint of existential psychology," *Harvard Educational Review, 32,* 1962, 403-415.

Von Fange, E. "Applications for school administration of the personality structure of educational personnel," Unpublished Doctoral Dissertation, University of Alberta, 1962.

Wallach, M. "Art, science, and representation: Toward an experimental psychology of aesthetics," *Journal of Aesthetics and Art Criticism, 18,* 1959, 159-73.

Witkin, H. *Personality through Perception.* New York: Harper and Row, 1954.

4

An Empirical Study of Cognitive Flexibility as a Dimension in the Selection and Evaluation of Counselor Effectiveness

The previous two chapters have developed the theory and the operational translations of cognitive flexibility. The purpose of this chapter is to present an empirical study of cognitive flexibility as a dimension in the selection and evaluation of counselor effectiveness.

The parallel research procedures employed in studies of teacher effectiveness (Emlaw, Mosher, Sprinthall, and Whiteley, 1963; Sprinthall, Mosher, and Whiteley, 1964; Sprinthall, Mosher, and Whiteley, 1966a), were presented in Chapter 2 of this book.

In reporting this empirical study, the first section is devoted to the research procedures.

The sample is described, including a brief account of the counselor training program context. Next we present the various procedures that we derived as a basis for predicting counselor performance—the Rorschach, the Thematic Apperception Test (TAT), the Personal Differentiation Test (PDT), the so-called "case" studies depicting counseling situations and a simulated counseling case (via a motion picture). This test battery, composed of three tests and two sets of simulated counseling situations, makes up the independent variables of the study. The dependent variable, the Counselor Rating Scale, was presented in detail in Chapter 3.

After describing the results of the study, we will discuss the relevance of these findings to counselor effectiveness, selection, training, and the implications for future research.

The Research Procedures

a) Selection of the Sample

The research was conducted with the cooperation of an Ed.M. (Master of Education) class in Guidance. The original population consisted of 25 students.

Of those 25 who were administered projective tests in the fall of 1964, before training began, 19 took the counseling practicum offered in the spring of 1965. Our sample. therefore, consisted of 19 students (seven men and 12 women) who completed the projective tests and other independent variables and for whom supervisory ratings were available.

b) The Counseling Training Program

The Master of Education degree in Guidance at Harvard is completed in one academic year. The typical program consists of an initial semester of course work in introduction to guidance theory, psychological theory of development, individual intelligence testing, and theory of counseling.

The spring term involves further course work in group tests, occupational-vocational development, and electives. A practicum in counseling is required. As part of this practicum, students spend an average of ten hours a week counseling in the schools. Supervision is provided in the field placement and through small group and individual supervision by the university faculty.

c) The Projective Test Scoring System

The projective tests (Rorschach and Thematic Apperception Test) were administered during the initial stages of the training program in the fall semester. The test protocols were coded and scored by the authors as a basis for making predictions on each dimension of the Counselor Rating Scale. The ratings were made, of course, independently of the actual counseling performance as rated by the supervisors.

The Rorschach was used in this study in such a manner as to develop a construct of the subject in the form of, "He seems like the sort of person who . . . " This method is based on McArthur's (1954) description of the approach of clinicians who were able to make the best predictions about an individual's behavior. Translated to predicting how an individual would counsel, the construct would take the form of, "He seems like the sort of person who would counsel . . . " This approach, using the Rorschach data, was applied to each flexible-rigid dimension in the rating scale (see appendix for a detailed presentation). A similar approach was employed in analyzing the stories from the TAT.

The procedures followed in scoring the Rorschach and the TAT (in somewhat modified form) were originally developed for the study parallel to this research which was presented in the foregoing chapter. Examples of flexible and rigid Rorschach and TAT responses are presented there.

d) The Personal Differentiation Test

The Personal Differentiation Test is a nonprojective measure of cognitive flexibility similar to the Role Construct Repertory Test (Kelly, 1955). The subject is required to consider the personal characteristics of particular individuals associated with the school environment. The stimulus content is six general names: "yourself," "best friend," "teacher," "principal," "underachiever," and "parents." These names are listed in groups of three, all possible combinations are included. The task is to link any two names of the three by a personal characteristic which differentiates the chosen two from the third. It is also required that a different characteristic be selected for each of the 20 sets. The responses were scored as indicating cognitive flexibility-rigidity on the basis of two general dimensions—a rating for the content of each item and a rating for all items.

e) The Case Studies

The two case studies used as predictive criteria were administered to the subjects early in the spring semester. The guidelines for rating these two cases were derived through discussions with counselor supervisors and experienced counselors. From the discussions the parameters were created—two categories for the case of John and four categories for the case of David. These categories were then scaled and the resultant scores provided a rank ordering of the subjects on the rigid-flexible continuum. The cases were developed as a type of "crisis" situation or "critical incident" in counseling. The subjects were asked to write out their responses as quickly as possible since the framework was created to see how quickly they could, in a sense, "think on their feet."

Case of John

The *Case of John* is illustrative:

As a counselor in a school, you have been seeing a student, John, on numerous occasions for what is sometimes called personal counseling. He is a very conscientious student, yet worried constantly about his academic work. These concerns have been the focus of the most recent sessions.

During the mid-term exam period, in fact, just a minute or two before he is to take his exam in history, he appears at your door. You look up from your work, with some surprise—you notice his eyes are moist as he struggles to say—"May I come in and see you?"

On the *Case of John*, subjects were asked to indicate: (1) what their specific response would be to the question and (2) their thoughts and feelings about the situation, particularly the dimensions they found troublesome as counselors.

From the point of view of scoring criteria, a *flexible response* generally would involve at least two dimensions: (a) *an acceptance* of the student in an "open" way and (b) a specific mention of *getting him to* the exam with an offer to see him after the exam. Ideally the counselor might offer to *go with* the boy and talk about the specifics of the exam as they go. Also the answer should mention the significance of the boy presenting himself to the counselor at this moment.

Examples of responses classified as flexible are the following:

(1) "After speaking briefly to him, I would arrange for him to come in after

the exam—he obviously wants to come to my office but that doesn't mean we can't be honest about the time he chose to come."

(2) "I would realize that in previous work in counseling we had not solved his problems and watch out that my own feelings of failure did not interfere— I would let him talk briefly—then walk him to the exam and remind him of our coming appointment for counseling."

The following responses were, by contrast, rated as rigid:

(1) The counselor gets trapped, seemingly caught in the dilemma with no way out.

"What can I give him in two minutes—Is it time for homely wisdom— or for what the 'nondirectives' consider taboo. 'You're not alone'"?

(2) A series of comments or questions which serve only to raise so much complexity that a resolution is either impossible or highly problematical:

"I would wonder why he was so upset—how to calm him down—to get him excused—would that be permitted—would it be best—would he consider himself different . . ."

(3) A response which might be classified as "instant diagnosis" or premature closure by the counselor:

"There is an attitude of basic insecurity here—I know he is well prepared and should take the exam."

(4) A response implying an inappropriate offer to the student. The counselor implicitly suggests that it might be possible to avoid the exam:

"Would it be better to make an appointment for us to talk after the exam?"

(5) A response in which there is an excessive concern that the student is trying to pull a "fast one." The counselor's response appears as excessively judgmental:

"I do not condone emotional upsets as a regular routine to avoid responsibility."

For more detailed instructions for scoring the *Case of John* see Appendix D.

Case of David

In the second case, the *Case of David,* a similar crisis situation was depicted:

Earlier in the day you had an initial counseling session with a college student. He came in, visibly upset, and literally poured out his feelings. He was very distraught with his academic studies. Although his record for the first two years was excellent, at the present time he is failing all his courses (at mid-term). He is a science major and is behind (at least one month) in his assignments for all his courses. He says he definitely wants to withdraw since he can't possibly catch up. Also he indicates that he has delayed seeing anyone about his difficulties because he felt he should handle things on his own—but admits somewhat ruefully that he tried to take all of his remaining science major requirements in this semester. Since it's Friday, you arrange to see him again on Monday for another session. As he's leaving he says that his father will probably phone you if it's all right. You agree. (You now learn that he called his father just before seeing you but was unable to say much of anything except that he wanted to withdraw). When you arrive home, there is a phone message and you soon find yourself talking with the student's father. He starts the conversation and very directly asks if you think his son should drop out.

On the *Case of David*, subjects were asked to indicate: (1) the main points of their reply to the father and (2) how this kind of situation brings the value question into focus, and what values they had represented in framing a reply to the student's father. For more detailed scoring instructions for the *Case of David* see Appendix E.

The flexible-rigid rating on the subject's response to the *Case of David* was based on four categories:

(1) *How the counseling role and function were presented to the father.* The scoring range was from explicitly defined through implicitly defined to undefined.

(2) *The specific response to the father's question in terms of the exploration of contingencies, options, or possibilities.*

Flexible	Rigid
Awareness that there are numerous possibilities:	Prescription of a specific course of action:
"He does have a number of possibilities open to him."	"With it so near the end of the term it is wise to drop a course rather than the whole program."
"There are certainly a number of alternatives at this time."	

(3) *The consistency of response.*

Flexible	Rigid
A response that is internally consistent:	A contradictory answer:
"I would try to explain to the father that I think this decision (on dropping out) is one that must be left to the boy. In my opinion, the father and I can be of help to the son—now that he has asked for help—by trying to explore	"There is no need to make the decision` immediately—perhaps I should discuss the pros and cons of dropping out with the student—Why don't you fly out—I feel it is worth it in the long run as it is a huge issue."

Flexible

what such a course of action
will entail, what the results
might be, and what possible
alternatives are open to him.
Both father and counselor
should try to encourage the
boy to take enough time to
think this thing through in
depth. But we cannot, and
should not, make the decision
for him."

(4) *The value orientation.* The value orientation dimension was evaluated in
terms of whether the student was seen as an individual who had to arrive at his own conclusions or whether the student ought to conform
automatically to some predefined institutional or societal norm.

(f) The Counseling Film

The film used in this study was *A Clinical Picture of Claustrophobia,* developed
by the Veterans' Administration (Finesinger and Powdermaker, 1951), in which
a counseling session is presented. It was shown to the subjects in the early part of
the spring term.

The film was stopped at 28 critical points following a procedure developed by
Strupp (1960). At each critical point the student was asked to respond to the client
as he thought appropriate or not to respond at all if he thought no response would
facilitate counseling.

Student responses were scored using a system developed by Allen (1966). The
focus is on that aspect of the client's verbalization to which the counselor chooses
to respond. Categories used in evaluating counselor response are as follows: response to feeling, such as recognition, question about, reorganization of, and response to unverbalized feeling; content, such as remarks about ideas, statements;
acceptance of client remark; interpretation; information giving; silence; and critical evaluation of the client, such as saying the client should be other than he is.
The results from the Allen scoring system were used to rate the array of counselor
responses and the appropriateness of the counselor response.

(g) Additional Test Data

In addition to the predictor variables enumerated above (the Rorschach, TAT,
PDT, and the simulated case studies) which we hypothesized would relate to the
dependent variable (supervisor's ratings of cognitive flexibility-rigidity), we also
included the test scores from the Graduate Record Exam or the Miller Analogies
Test. Although we made no specific predictions, we did include the scores in our
analysis to ascertain if there was any trend or possible relationship between these

intellectual measures and either the independent or dependent variables. The intellectual test data could be considered as a possible correlate variable.

(b) Criteria for Counselor Effectiveness—The Counselor Rating Blank: The Dependent Variable

(1) *Description:* The rating scale is designed to categorize and rate certain characteristics of counselor behavior. This is presented in detail in Appendix B.

(2) *Use in the Present Study:* The ratings of counselor behavior for the experimental sample were made by the Harvard Supervisors. The ratings were based on a five month period of supervision involving counseling tapes, verbal and written reports, weekly seminars, and individual supervision sessions at least every other week.

Rating of counseling behavior obviously involves an inferential and evaluative process by the supervisor. As previously noted, the Counselor Rating Scale used in this study provides examples of specific flexible and rigid counseling behaviors for each sub-scale. The purpose is to focus the rating process on counseling behaviors hypothesized as indices of the organizing flexibility-rigidity construct. This serves, hopefully, to reduce intuitive ratings and increase the possibility of replication studies. Any formal control for rater reliability was felt to be premature at this stage of the research.

(i) Reliability

Certain of the instruments used in this study lend themselves more readily to the standard methods of estimating reliability than do the projective-type data. As retest data were not available, coefficients of equivalence rather than stability were derived (Cronbach, 1960) when the data were appropriate.

The critical-incident casework consisted of two forms administered a week apart. When correlated, the rank scores from the two cases yielded an equivalence coefficient of $+.72$, which is significant beyond the .005 level. Interjudge reliability was estimated by having the two judges score independently the responses of six subjects randomly chosen. The correlation between ranks assigned after scoring was $+.88$ for one case and $+.91$ for the other ($p < .02$ for both).

As the Personal Differentiation Test was administered only once, an internal-consistency procedure was used. Each test was scored in two parts, odd numbered questions yielding one set of scores and even numbered questions marked independently providing a second set. The coefficient of equivalence was $+.94$ ($p < .05$).

The responses to the movie film were subjected to an interjudge reliability estimate. Two judges independently scored the protocols according to a procedure developed by Allen (1966). A rank order correlation between the two sets of scores yielded a rho coefficient of $+.94$ ($p < .01$)

The scores derived from the projective test procedures (the Rorschach and the Thematic Apperception Test) were not tested for reliability. Data elicited from projective instruments are amenable to tests for reliability only under certain con-

ditions—by retesting subjects, by "blind" scoring procedures, or by scoring protocols in separate sections. Because our method for scoring the projective test responses attempted to combine a standard "sign" interpretation with clinical inferences made during the test administered, the conditions for reliability testing
did not hold. By specifying a series or constellation of "signs," as indicated in the
appendix, along each dimension to be predicted, we attempted to outline the
major aspects of the subjects' responses which formed the basis for our predictions.
Two examiners discussed each protocol in terms of such elements and then pooled
these judgments as a base for the predictions.*

The supervisor ratings were analyzed for an estimate of internal consistency.
The ratings were made by each supervisor along each dimension of the Counselor Rating Scale. The overall scores were correlated with the scores on each of
the eight sub-scales of the Counselor Rating Scale. The rank order coefficients
ranged from +.91 to +.95.

As the intellective data were the results of performance on standardized tests—
the Graduate Record Exam or the Miller Analogies Test—reliability for these instruments was not reconfirmed.

Results

Table 6 presents the rank correlation coefficients for three of the four predictors
in this study. Two predictors, projective test scores and scores on the critical-incident cases, correlate highly with each other ($r = .72$, $p < .01$) as well as with the
criterion variable, the supervisors' ratings. The correlation coefficients were +.78
between the projective test scores and the supervisors' ratings, and +.73 between
the critical-incident scores and the criterion. The scores on the Personal Differentiation Test tended to cluster in the upper half of the scoring range, and the
relationships between the rank order of these scores and the criterion variable
were insignificant.

TABLE 6

Rank Correlation Coefficients between Predictors and the Criterion Variable

Predictors	Supervisors' Ratings
Projective Tests	+.78 p < .005 n = 19
Critical-Incident Cases	+.73 p < .005 n = 19
Personal Differentiation Test	+.33 p n.s. n = 15

---

* We have used this procedure for projective test ratings in three different research samples, as described in the discussion section of this report. In each case the predictions have been relatively
accurate indicators of flexibility-rigidity. In predicting effective *versus* ineffective role performance
by teachers, counselors, etc., an area of research that has proven remarkably resistant to more "objective" assessment procedures, we felt some justification in adopting the clinical inference model for
our predictions.

The fourth predictor was a film, *A Clinical Picture of Claustrophobia*, the data from which provided three arrays of scores: (1) the number of response categories, (2) the number of "feeling" responses, and (3) the number of "content" responses elicited from each subject. Rank correlation between the supervisors' ratings and the number of response categories yielded a near zero coefficient, as was also the case with the number of feeling responses. Between the criterion and the number of content responses there was a negative correlation ($r = -.47$, $p < .025$). Overall, however, the absolute number of responses of a given type did not correlate with the criterion.

To determine if the relative frequency of a response type was related to the supervisors' ratings, a ratio of the number of "feeling" responses to the number of "content" responses was derived. Subjects were classified as to whether the feeling/content ratio was greater or less than one, and then compared to the supervisors' ratings in three categories of flexibility-rigidity. Table 7 shows that the relative frequency of occurrence of a response type is related to the criterion ($x^2 = 8.42, df = 2, p < .02$).

TABLE 7

Movie Film Response: Feeling/Content Ratios
Compared to Supervisors' Ratings

	$\frac{\text{Feeling}}{\text{Content}}$	Ratio > 1	$\frac{\text{Feeling}}{\text{Content}}$	Ratio < 1
Supervisors' Ratings	Above average (most flexible)	8		0
	Average	2		2
	Below average (least flexible)	2		5

df = 2x^2 = 8.42 p < .02

A final variable included in the analysis for control purposes was that of intellectual ability. The supervisors' ratings and the intellective data correlated only .09; that is, there was no relationship between scores on the Miller Analogies Test or the Graduate Record Exam and the supervisors' ratings of rigidity-flexibility in counseling.

Discussion

The major finding of this study was that cognitive flexibility-rigidity as predicted on the basis of projective tests demonstrated a reasonably high positive relationship to supervisors' ratings on the same dimension. The correlation coefficient of +.78 accounts for over one-half of the variance in rated performance of counselors in training by supervisors using the Counselor Rating Scales.

It is particularly noteworthy that this is the third time that such a finding has appeared. With a similar methodology to predict and evaluate teacher effectiveness on the basis of cognitive flexibility-rigidity, analogous results have been derived —once with a sample of teacher trainees at the elementary school level (Emlaw, Mosher, Sprinthall, and Whiteley, 1963) and more recently with a sample of secondary level teacher trainees (Chapter 2 above). Using a scoring system for responses on the Rorschach and the Thematic Apperception Test based on indices of flexibility-rigidity, a consistent relationship has been demonstrated between these indices and role performance of both counselors and teachers in training.

By focusing on behavioral definitions of counselor role we have adopted a proximate criterion of counselor performance. This point should be underscored. There is no "hard" evidence that a counselor who behaves in accord with the proposed model will promote effective change within pupils. Until research in counseling outcome becomes more advanced, especially in terms of specifying the array of criteria which are appropriate, it will continue to be necessary to develop adequate proximate measures.

The second major finding of the study was that the scores on the critical-incident case episodes were statistically significant when correlated with the supervisors' ratings. In fact, the actual correlation of +.73 was only slightly less in magnitude than the correlation between the projective tests and the criterion measure. There does seem to be a reasonably strong logical interpretation for this finding. By design the cases represented incidents where there was no single correct answer and where, indeed, to be prescriptive would tend to close off exploration. The ambiguous nature of the problems could most appropriately be handled if the counselor was relatively open-ended in his responses. This kind of a test is a paper and pencil laboratory situation bearing close similarities to the demands of actual counseling situations that the apprentice might confront. Obviously there is also a close connection between all that is implied here and cognitive flexibility. The need to think and respond quickly while in the situation may have been the most important element in apparently differentiating between the counselors subsequently judged flexible versus those judged rigid by their counseling supervisors.

A third major finding given current admissions practices was that the traditional methods of selecting graduate students—the Miller Analogies and Graduate Record Exam—correlated only +.09 with supervisors' ratings of competence as a counselor. This is not to say that an intellectual ability sufficient to master graduate level work is not a critical requirement. The MAT or GRE can serve us well as cutoff scores below which successful completion of graduate study is problematic. But we should not delude ourselves that we are predicting counseling effectiveness.

It might be very worthwhile in light of the above finding to research the possibility of critical-incident cases as a relevant criterion for admission. The findings, however, were based on graduate students in training and cannot be applied to admissions candidates as selection devices until their feasibility and validity is determined by administering them before coursework has begun.

The research findings taken together raise an extremely important question. If, as has been indicated, the predictions were relatively accurate, does this mean that cognitive flexibility-rigidity is relatively "fixed" in advance of graduate training? While the research design was not established with a view of systematically investigating this question, several clinical impressions emerged which merit comment.

We found a small but tenacious minority to have such an overdetermined rigidity that despite all supervision efforts to the contrary over the course of a year, they remained as rigid as they had been at the beginning. And because they had in the process acquired a range of words and phrases which sounded reasonable and professionally appropriate, their rigidity was all the more deceptive and perhaps destructive.

There was a group of students whose personal qualities made flexibility a natural method of approach to a wide variety of problems. Besides being a pleasure to have in supervision, they were more effective as counselors beginning training than many of the other students were, regrettably, at the end of their training. Fortunately, these flexible and effective students were clearly identifiable by the predictive measures.

The remaining students constituted a middle group and represent an important area for future research. They turned out by and large to be reasonably effective. They generally had a more difficult time learning to be counselors. They probably never will be as outstanding as the clearly more flexible group. But they can learn to be more than journeyman counselors. It will be necessary to focus on methods of supervision and their impact on this group as a future research problem. Equally important for future research is the identification of the characteristics of those counselors who make major moves toward increased flexibility and those who make minimal progress.

BIBLIOGRAPHY

Allen, T. "Counselors in training: A study of role effectiveness as a function of psychological openness." Unpublished Doctoral Dissertation, Harvard University, 1966.

Cronbach, L. *Essentials of Psychological Testing.* 2nd ed. New York: Harper and Row, 1960.

Emlaw, R., R. Mosher, N. Sprinthall, and J. Whiteley. "Teacher effectiveness: A method for prediction and evaluation," *The National Elementary Principal*, November, 1963.

Finesinger, J., and F. Powdermaker. *A Clinical Picture of Claustrophobia* (film). Washington, D. C.: Veterans Administration, 1951.

McArthur, C. "Analyzing the clinical process," *Journal of Counseling Psychology*, 4, 1954, 203-206.

Sprinthall, N., J. Whiteley, and R. Mosher. "Prediction and evaluation of teacher effectiveness at the secondary school level," Cooperative Research Project, No. S-143. U. S. Office of Education, Department of Health, Education, and Welfare. Washington, D. C., 1964.

Sprinthall, N., J. Whiteley, and R. Mosher. "A study of teacher effectiveness," *Journal of Teacher Education, XVIII*, Spring 1966a, No. 1, 93-106.

Sprinthall, N., J. Whiteley, and R. Mosher. "Cognitive flexibility as a dimension of counselor behavior: Definition, rationale, research focus," *Counselor Education and Supervision, V*, No. 4, Summer 1966b, 188-197.

Strupp, H. H. *Psychotherapists in Action*. New York: Grune and Stratton, 1960.

SECTION III

PSYCHOLOGICAL OPENNESS AS A DIMENSION OF COUNSELOR EFFECTIVENESS

5

Psychological Openness in Psychological Theory

One of the cardinal admonitions put to aspiring counselors is the Socratic dictum "Know Thyself." Indeed, sensitivity to one's own psychological characteristics, to one's own thoughts, feelings, and fantasies, what might be called "psychological openness," seems to find its way into virtually every list of desiderata to be sought in the personalities of prospective counselors, e.g., American Psychological Association Committee on Counselor Training 1952, American Psychological Association Committee on Training in Clinical Psychology 1947, Feder 1961, Weitz 1957.

Although the term "psychological openness" is new, the concept is not. It has relatively short but respectable lineage. Recent literature has underscored the importance of distinguishing among persons in terms of the access they have to their own impulses, their own feelings, their less socialized and reality-bound ideas. While a continuum is clearly implied, the concept is most generally defined in terms of its hypothetical extremes—"psychological openness" and "psychological closedness."

For example, Rokeach (1960) marshalls an appreciable amount of evidence in support of his hypothesis that "openness" and "closedness" are important qualities of belief systems. One of the most cruicial properties of the "open system" is, for Rokeach, the extensiveness of the communication among the various parts of the system. This intra-system communication is not found in "closed systems." Rokeach contends, further, that belief systems are excellent models of personality (1960, p. 7). Consequently, by clear implication, "openness" and "closedness" appear as significant aspects of personality. And, by extension, the "open person" is one in whom there is a relatively high degree of self-communication. The "closed person" is one in whom there is a greater degree of isolation among the various levels and/or varieties of his experience.

Sprinthall, Whiteley, and Mosher (1963, 1964, 1966a, 1966b, 1967) have expanded Rokeach's notions. They have found meaningful relationships between the placement of subjects along a similar dimension ("flexibility—rigidity") and performance as teachers (Chapter 2) and counselors (Chapter 4). "Flexibility," as defined by these authors, seems to entail an awareness by the person of the nature of his internal reactions to cues in the environment. On the other hand, persons designated "rigid" by this scheme appear, in part, to be those who strive to minimize the variety of cues contained in their experience.

Getzels and Jackson discriminate between persons demonstrating "profound personal introspectiveness," those who explore their own fantasy freely, and those who "focus only on the means and ends of everyday existence" (1962, p. 102; p. 105). Bruner (1962) and Barron (1963) differentiate persons according to the range of experience they permit into consciousness. At one extreme, they place persons who rigidly exclude very few thoughts and who entertain a wide range of impulses and ideas. At the other extreme, they place persons in whom there is a major suppression of thought, particularly of thoughts and feelings related to impulses.

Schachtel has stated that "openness in the encounter with the world means that one's sensibilities are more freely receptive to new reflections of the world and its objects" (1959, pp. 241f.). At the opposite pole, new experience is strenuously avoided; conventional labels and ways of construing the world are assiduously guarded (Schachtel, 1959, pp. 185f.). According to Carl Rogers, for a person at one end of this continuum, "every stimulus is freely relayed through the nervous system without being distorted by a process of defensiveness. Whether the stimulus originates in the environment . . . or whether it originates in the viscera, or as a memory trace in the central nervous system it is available to awareness" (1961, p. 353). At the other end of the continuum, Rogers contends, a person carefully screens all sensory input—particularly that from internal sources —to obviate the recognition of those thoughts and feelings which evoke anxiety. Similarly, Maslow (1959) divided a group of subjects which he studied intensively into two groups in terms of this dimension. The members of the group that would be labeled "psychologically open," according to the present terminology, were characterized by a "lack of fear of their own insides, of their own impulses, emotions, thoughts . . ." (1959, p. 88). The members of the other group, the "psychologically closed" group, as it were, "walled off through fear much that lay within themselves. They controlled, they inhibited, they repressed and they suppressed. They disapproved of their deeper selves and expected that others did, too" (1959, p. 88).

It is averred by the foregoing authors that psychological openness has more adaptive value than psychological closedness. According to Dollard and Miller (1950), psychologically open persons can use their impulses, their emotions, and thoughts to enrich their view of the world, to divert themselves, or, they may suppress them as inappropriate according to the realistic demands of their current situation. In these persons, thoughts and feelings are pursued or suppressed according to their relevance to their purposes. By contrast, psychologically closed persons tend to exclude certain areas of thought systematically regardless of their pertinence to the realization of personal goals (Dollard and Miller, 1950; Kubie, 1958; Getzels and Jackson, 1961, p. 129).

Thus it is clear that the term psychological openness has reference to a personality datum of recognized importance. Further, the preceding descriptions of the concept's polarities serve to strengthen our purchase on it. As a result, a somewhat more satisfactory definition of psychological openness may be promulgated: The placement of a person along a continuum from psychological openness to psychological closedness is determined by the degree to which he is able to use his personal experience— his impulses, his feelings, his fantasies—for adaptive purposes. The greater this capacity, the closer the person would be placed to the psychologically open pole of the continuum.

The rationale for such a prerequisite for counseling practice depends largely upon two general arguments. The first asserts that psychological openness is an essential precondition to the understanding of the thoughts and feelings of others. On one hand, it is claimed, psychological closedness leads to distortion in interpersonal perception. On the other hand, one's own thoughts and feelings are held to provide important clues to those of others. The second general argument avers that psychological openness is crucial to the establishment of an interpersonal atmosphere conducive to client self-exploration.

Summary

In this section the term "psychological openness" was introduced. The position of the concept to which the term refers in psychological theory was examined. Considerable agreement was found among a number of leading theorists in regard to the centrality of the concept to the understanding of personality. The definition of psychological openness was further clarified by reference to this literature.

Arguments supporting the claim that psychological openness is an important variables in counseling performance were stated.

The following section examines the first of these arguments.

Some Effects of Psychological Closedness

Virtually every theory of counseling places a premium on the counselor's ability to understand important aspects of a client's perception of his situation (Allen, 1964). In this section, the evidence bearing on the effect of a lack of psychological openness (psychological closedness) upon such understanding will be examined. Empirical investigations of the relationship between the misperception of oneself and the misperception of other persons will be reviewed.

The Personal Equation

As the astronomer of an earlier age rendered his observations more accurate by introducing a correction for his personal reaction time, it is held that the counselor must be aware of his own biases, his own psychological "sore spots," lest serious distortions creep into his understanding of others.

It is generally assigned to Freud's credit that he was the first to give systematic attention to the effects of the therapist's personality on his perception of patients (Jones, 1955, p. 231). From observations of the therapist's all-too-human proclivity to distort concurrent interpersonal relationships in terms of his personal conflicts (counter-transference), the training analysis took its place in the psychoanalytic curriculum (Strupp, 1960, p. 290). Wrote Freud,

> It is not enough for this that he (the analyst) himself should be an approximately normal person. It may be insisted, rather, that he should have undergone a psychoanalytic purification and have become aware of those complexes of his own which would be apt to interfere with his grasp of what the patient tells him . . . Every unresolved repression in him constitutes what has been aptly described by Stekel as a "blind spot" in his analytic perception (Freud, 1957, V.XII, p. 116).

Psychoanalytic writers since Freud have joined in support of the training or "didactic" analysis as an essential part of the analyst's training regimen on precisely these grounds (Fenichel, 1945; Putnam, 1912; Knight, 1953). Likewise, Hartmann has asserted that "every instance of self-deception is accompanied by a misjudgment of the external world as well" (1958, p. 64).

Neither has this emphasis been restricted to analysts. Fifty per cent of a random sample of 500 members of Division 12 (clinical psychology) of the American Psychological Association gave an unqualified positive response to the question, "Should some form of personal therapy be required of all student therapists?" (Lubin, 1965), ostensibly for the same reason. Tyler, in a book on general counseling, maintains that personal counseling is a potentially useful experience for the counselor because:

> It helps the counselor to know where his own biases and sensitive areas are (1961, p. 243).

Similarly, the Code of Ethics of the American Psychological Association warns that the psychological counselor must be:

> aware of the inadequacies of his own personality which may bias his appraisal of others or distort his relationships with them . . . (American Psychological Association, 1953, pp. 45f).

Rogers (1951) offers an account of this phenomenon. As he sees it, people, including counselors, tend to block off or dissociate experiences which are alarmingly incongruent with important aspects of their conception of themselves. The experiences are not allowed a place in the language system of the person and are thereby kept out of awareness. However, vigilance must constantly be maintained to obviate the ever present threat that these damaging experiences will be brought to mind.

> Words and behaviors are attacked because they represent or resemble the feared experiences. There is no real understanding of (an) other as a separate person, since he is perceived mostly in terms of threat or nonthreat to the self (Rogers, 1951, pp. 520f).

That is, in order to avoid being reminded of experiences which are inimical to his image of himself, a person may unwittingly mispercieve related material in regard to others.

Thus, on the theoretical level there are grounds for asserting that a lack of openness to one's own thoughts and feelings is detrimental to the understanding of others. Let us turn to the empirical findings. There is indeed some experimental confirmation to the notion that personality factors influence interpersonal perception. Murray (1933) found that children who were exposed to a game of "murder," rated pictures of faces as being more "malicious" than they had before the game. Sears (1936) discovered that his subjects, 100 college men, tended to rate their fellows more inaccurately on personality traits in regard to which they were judged to lack insight into themselves. In Posner's study (1940) children who felt guilty over an act of "selfishness" attributed more selfishness to others than did guiltless controls. Later studies are somewhat equivocal; some support the findings of the foregoing work, that personality factors affect interpersonal perception, e.g., Taft (1950), Rokeach (1945), Green (1948), Dymond (1948), Adams (1927). Others, e.g., Lemann and Soloman (1952), Frenkel-Brunswik (1942), failed to do so.

Blum's ingenious study (1963) seems to bear even more directly on the "blind spot" hypothesis. His subjects were 17 advanced graduate students in clinical psychology. He attempted to identify areas of psychological conflict in his subjects by means of the "Blacky Pictures" (Blum, 1950). This projective technique involves the use of cartoons which depict dogs in acts corresponding to the "psychosexual stages" of development outlined by psychoanalytic theory. The subjects were all well-acquainted with the technique and its theoretical underpinnings. The experimental tasks set for them in several individual sessions were, first, to name and describe each of the eleven Blacky Pictures and its psychosexual referent and, second, some weeks later, to name the pictures as quickly as possible. Subsequently, they were asked to rank the pictures according to the extent to which each of the areas they represented was a problem to them. The clustering of errors, omissions, long pauses, perseverations, and peculiar responses on particular cards were taken as indications of conflict there.

The subjects were then presented with brief tachistoscopic exposures of four of the 11 cards and asked to identify the picture shown in each case. None of the subjects discovered that only four of the pictures were actually employed.

Postman (1953), attacked the notion of "perceptual defense," discounting evidence that conflict relevant material is perceptually "repressed" or "screened out." Rather, he suggested, apparent "vigilance" or "defense" could be accounted for more "parsimoniously" in terms of nondefensive response preferences.

If this were so, Blum reasoned, subjects would simply make nonconflictual responses more frequently than conflictual ones. Consequently, the difference between the number of times conflict-laden pictures not actually exposed were called should be as great as the difference between the number of calls of conflict-laden pictures and the nonconflict pictures shown. That is, if only responses and not perceptual tendencies were involved, the presence or absence of pictures from the perceptual task would have no appreciable effect on the results.

Blum's findings were to the contrary. While the mean number of calls for both categories of the absent pictures (both conflictual and neutral) were almost identical, the difference between the means for the conflict pictures used and the nonconflict pictures used was highly significant ($p<.001$). Thus, it seems, the defensive behavior took place on the perceptual level, against stimuli in the immediate environment (Blum, 1963, p. 153). It should further be noted that as a group the subjects were able to identify the pictures shown beyond a chance level despite their disclaimers. This clearly suggests that the process involved may take place without awareness on the part of the perceiver.

Blum's results lend support to the concept of perceptual defense:

> Subjects predisposed to use the mechanism of repression in conjunction with a given conflict will, when confronted subliminally with a conflict-relevant stimulus, show defensive behavior directly traceable to the perceptual process itself (1963, p. 154).

These findings seem to neutralize the force of some of Postman's objections. They provide support for the assertion that the veridicality of perception may be reduced by the unwitting attempt of the perceiver to avoid an encounter with conflict-relevant material.

Striber (1961) set out explicitly to test Rogers' formulation. He hypothesized that distortions in interpersonal perception would occur in areas where a discrepancy obtained between the perceiver's concept of himself and others' opinions of him. To test this hypothesis, Striber had 153 student nurses make self and ideal-self ratings on various personality dimensions. Each subject then rated herself as she thought others would rate her. She also rated five classmates she liked and five nonassociates whom she had met in the class. As anticipated, Striber found that subjects tended to overrate others on those undesirable traits where their self-ratings were at odds with the ratings given them by others and there was only minimal awareness of this discrepancy.

Finally, Cutler (1958) tested the notion that areas of intrapersonal conflict in the counselor create "blind spots" that interfere with his perception of clients most directly. Personal conflicts were again identified through the comparison of counselors' self-ratings with ratings made of them by acquaintances. Where the self-ratings deviated widely from the consensus of the acquaintances, a conflict was assumed to exist.

Counselors' process notes of counseling were compared with tape-recordings of the same sessions. A counselor was said to have distorted an issue when he either under- or over-reported it in his notes. Twenty-eight of 40 predictions made from the hypothesis were completely confirmed; two others were in the right direction. There were insufficient data concerning four predictions, and six were without verification.

Discussion of the Research

The foregoing research investigates the claim arising from clinical work that a counselor's lack of insight into himself interferes with his perception of clients. Of course, as with virtually any inquiry pioneering in a complex and controversial area, there are questions which may be raised.

One of the most important questions is that in regard to the questionnaire technique employed by many investigators, e.g., Sears (1936) and Striber (1961), to assess the accuracy of subjects' interpersonal perceptions and self-insights. In these cases, accuracy was defined in terms of the agreement between the subject's predictions of the responses of other subjects to a rating device and their actual responses. Self-insight was determined by comparing a subject's self-rating with a consensus of those made of him by his peers. Since subjects whose predictions of the responses of others were most accurate also tended to rate themselves similarly to the way in which others rated them, it was concluded that self-insight and accuracy in the perception of others are related.

Unhappily, the data lend themselves to an alternative interpretation as well. In view of Cronbach's (1955) analysis of such procedures, one might suppose that these results may be a function of the consistency of subjects' response sets in regard to the scales involved. Thus, if a subject consistently gave higher or lower ratings on both scales than the majority of his peers, he would appear to be low both in self-insight and in interpersonal accuracy. In fact, however, his predictions may discriminate well among the subjects he judged. Likewise, if a subject restricted himself to the middle range of the scale, rating very conservatively, he would appear to be acute in both regards even though his ratings were of no value in differentiating among subjects. His accuracy score would be greatly inflated by the fact that by rating conservatively, restricting his ratings to the most commonly chosen points on the scale, he would make no gross errors.

In Sears' study there is no way of knowing that this artifact did not contribute wholly or in part to his results. However, in Striber's case, the situation is a bit different. Striber specifies that subjects will *overrate* in others what they *underrate* in themselves. Therefore, while a response set might, in this case, obscure results compatible with his hypothesis, it would not produce spuriously significant ones. For example, if a subject consistently favored high points on the scale, he would tend to overrate *both* himself and others on unfavorable characteristics; hence, the anticipated discrepancy would not be detected.

Further, the ability of such ratings to predict errors in interpersonal perception (Cutler, 1958) supports the inferences concerning the relationship of self-insight and interpersonal perception that Sears and Striber drew from their data. Nevertheless, it is to be hoped that further inquiry will be made along these lines and that it will include controls for response set.[1] It also must be noted that there is urgent need for a replication of Cutler's study with a larger sample and with some further clarification of the statistical model employed.

However, the general convergence of the experimental results along the lines predicted by clinical theory makes a promising hypothesis that unacknowledged feelings and conflicts influence the perception of other persons. At very least, it is one deserving further study.

Some Contributions of Psychological Openness to the Counseling Process

In this section several contributions of psychological openness to the counseling process will be examined. The theoretical relationship between openness and interpersonal understanding will be reconsidered in terms of the positive contribution of the former to the latter. The empirical findings relevant to these formulations will be presented. The role of the psychological openness of the counselor in the creation of the therapeutic atmosphere will be discussed in regard to the available experimental evidence.

Understanding the Client: Hypothesis Formation

The contribution of psychological openness to interpersonal understanding goes far beyond the introduction of error by psychological constriction or closedness. Its contribution has a positive facet which is probably of greater moment than the negative one involved in distortion.

Bakan points to it in the attempt to answer the question—how is it possible for a counselor to have any idea as to what is going on in the client's mind? Bakan asserts that the richness and variety of the counselor's own emotional experience are basic factors of the first order in the process of understanding another. Thus, he holds it to be crucial "that (the counselor's) training shall open up to consciousness the wide range of experience that lie within him" (1956, p. 661).

---

[1] The statistical controls employed by Bronfenbrenner *et al.* (1958) offer one possibility.

Bordin carries this thought a bit further:

> In order to fully understand what it means to be helpless or to be in
> a rage, and how it feels when some other person turns away from you
> when you feel helpless or when someone tells you to calm down when
> you feel in a rage, the observer must draw upon his own experience
> (Bordin, 1955, p. 173).

Leif (1960), Dellis (1960), and Menninger et al. (1963) make similar asserva-
tions. Weigart contends that understanding of the client is to be had "only if
(the counselor) gives up the illusion of artificial neutrality and becomes fully aware
of his own emotional reactions" (1961, p. 92).

To grasp more fully the contentions of these writers it seems necessary that a
brief look be taken at the process by which a counselor is thought to achieve some
understanding of the emotional communications of clients. To do so, attention
must be turned to the work of theorists with a psychoanalytic bent, e.g., Fliess
(1942); Greenson (1954); Katz (1963); Knight (1953); Reik (1948); Shafer
(1959). Others, such as Bruner and Tagiuri (1954); Brofenbrenner (1958); Taft
(1950); Tagiuri and Petrullo (1958), have written at length on the subject of
interpersonal perception. However, their discussions have largely been limited to
methodological problems involved in its measurement. Further, their concern has
been primarily with the accuracy with which casual acquaintances could specify
each other's surface attitudes to the neglect of intensive interactions such as that
between counselor and client. The former group of authors, on the other hand,
have focused on the understanding of important emotional reactions. They, unfortunately, speak in terms of "projection," "identification," "introjection," "the
enlargement of ego boundaries." Nonetheless, their basic conceptions can be
stated briefly as follows:

As a counselor interacts with a client, he obtains information about him
through a myriad of verbal and behavioral cues. Taken with whatever additional
information is available from other sources, general observation, the nature of
the work the subject does, the communications of acquaintances, he can place
himself imaginatively in the client's position to some degree i.e., imagine that
certain conditions of life which apply to the client apply for a moment to him.
He then has recourse to his own feelings, his own inclinations in such a situation,
to generate hypotheses concerning those of the client. For many writers, this step
is the crux of the process. Murray, for example, holds that the process of understanding is essentially a:

> process whereby an observer experiences the feelings or emotions which
> in his personality are associated (1) with the situation in which the
> subject is placed, or (2) with the forms of behavior the subject exhi-
> bits (1938, p. 745).

Fenichel indicates that understanding "consists of two acts: (a) an identification with the other person, and (b) an awareness of one's own feelings after the identification and in this way an awareness of the object's feelings" (1945, p. 511). In Fliess' words, the empathizer imagines that he is in the subject's place and attends to the strivings that well up in him as a result.

> He then projects the striving, after he has "tested it," back on to the patient and so finds himself in possession of inside knowledge of (his) nature, having thereby, acquired the emotional basis for his interpretation (1942, p. 215).[2]

From this "inside knowledge" the counselor constructs what Greenson (1961) calls a "model" of the other. This consists of an integration of the experiential and situational data now available to him concerning the subject. The counselor then returns to his further experience with him to test out the validity of his "model," the validity of the inferences that flow from it, and to make whatever revisions seem now to be required:

> Observing a patient's life at any one point, we tentatively project on to him the feelings we once felt under similar circumstances, and then test this projection by further observation (Schafer, 1959, p. 347).

Similarly, Tyler, writing for counselors outside the analytic tradition, offers the following:

> From the moment he first encounters a client, a counselor begins to form what may be called a "working image" of the person. What he finds out through interviews, tests, observations, and background sources serves to modify this image, filling in details, making it more complex and accurate (Tyler, 1961, p. 63).

Thus, as Meehl (1954) and McArthur (1954; 1956) point out, the process closely approximates the classical paradigm of the scientific method (Kaplan, 1964). Hypotheses are formed: predictions are deduced from them and tested. The hypotheses are then modified in terms of the findings. McArthur (1956)

---

[2] Rapaport, Schafer, and Gill (1946) and Solley and Murphy (1960) make similar points in regard to general perceptual functioning. Rapaport *et al.* stress the central importance of "freedom and mobility of the associative processes" to adaptive perceptual behavior (1946, p. 94). They write of the "cogwheeling of associations into reality" (1946, p. 92). By this they mean that the associations— the recollections of past experience—which sensory data may trigger provide a context for meaning for them. At the same time, of course, constant reference to sense data gives an adaptive focus to the associative process.

Solley and Murphy (1960), in a similar vein, emphasize the contribution which stimuli from internal sources make to the perception of external phenomena. They assert that "to the extent an individual can learn to discern and recognize these (internal) cues, he will gain greater control over his perceptual system, and hence, become more veridical in his perceptions" (1960, p. 260).

further notes that in the Adult Development Study at Harvard,[3] those experts who drew hypotheses from their own experiences, from inner promptings, were clearly superior to those whose predictions represented deductions from theoretical principles.

Finally, it should be noted that this conception of the process of interpersonal sensitivity is a most widely held one. Indeed, it may be shown that the aggressively nonpsychoanalytic theories of Sarbin, Taft, and Baily (1960) and Allport (1937) are perfectly compatible with it (Allen, 1964).

Conclusion

The implications of the theory seem clear. First, one's awareness of his own feelings in a wide range of situations is a necessary point of departure from which any real understanding of the emotions of another person can occur. It is an indispensible source of "hypotheses" concerning what the other may be experiencing. As Menninger puts it, the counselor's:

> own previous experience with such love, wistfulness, disappointment, sorrow, anger, and fear enables him to understand the present emotions of the patient, displaced and presently inappropriate as they are (Menninger *et al.*, 1963, p. 630).

These "hypotheses" are not, however, in themselves sufficient for understanding. Indeed, taken alone without careful consideration of the difference obtaining between the client and himself, they may be a source of serious distortion. Thus, "the free availability of memories[4] (which the counselor has of his own emotional experience) must be supplemented by the sensing and judging of similarities that bear on their relevance to the client's situation" (Schafer, 1959, p. 348).

As a result, the sensitive counselor may be supposed, in the first place, to be a person who has free access to his emotional experience. But, in the second place, while he is capable of *enriching* his view of the world by means of hypotheses

---

3 In the Adult Development Study, experts were asked to predict the courses of the lives of Harvard students in the ten-year period following their graduation from extensive personal data gathered during their matriculation. The predictions were compared with comprehensive follow-up data.

4 It is important to keep in mind that the feelings upon which the sensitive counselor draws are thought to be noncontemporaneous or greatly attentuated; they have a definite "as if" quality. Thus Fliess (1942) has reference to "experimental fantasies" and Reik (1948) speaks of "embryonic feelings" to differentiate them from fullblown feeling states which the counselor shares with the client. The distinction is crucial. For it is difficult indeed to see how a counselor can be of maximum assistance to the client if he is caught up in the same web of emotion as the client. Hence, Rogers (1942) advises counselors "to sense the client's anger, fear, or confusion as if it were your own, *yet without your own anger, fear, or confusion getting bound up in it*" (1942, p. 284). (Emphasis provided.)

drawn from most personal feelings and fantasies, he does not cut his experience to fit them; neither does he substitute them for reality. He is psychologically open. [5]

Research Findings

Turning now from theory to research, one finds several studies which bear on this widely accepted principle of clinical practice; that psychological openness is an important precondition of sensitivity to others.

The first line of evidence supports the underlying assumption that sensitivity to the feelings of others depends, at least in part, on relatively stable personality characteristics of the counselor. Ellsworth (1962; 1963) analyzed the degree of consistency with which counselor-trainees responded to feeling in counseling and noncounseling situations. Samples of the subjects' verbal behavior taken from counseling sessions and from class discussions were scored for amount of feeling-verbalization. The results supported Ellsworth's predictions. The rank which a subject attained for feeling-verbalization in counseling was closely related to that which he received in the noncounseling situation (tau = .49; p = .0007).

Thus, sensitivity to feeling appears to be something more than a cloak which the would-be counselor may don when he confronts a client. The implication is that it is a function of important personality variables. What then is the evidence that psychological openness is such a variable?

Kagan (1961) found that subjects who showed a definite tendency to think of people in terms of thoughts and feelings were significantly more open to their own affects than those who concerned themselves with the more external attributes of people. The 64 adults who served as subjects were given a thematic apperception test, an inkblot test, a tachistoscopic presentation of figures, and a sorting task involving pictures of people. The thematic apperception tests were scored for the amount of reference made to the affects of the story characters. The inkblot responses were scored for the amount of human movement, and the sorting task for groupings for which affect terms were given as a rationale, e.g., "these three pictures go together because all three look sad." All of these scores were significantly intercorrelated so as to suggest, in agreement with Ellsworth, that a relatively stable personality variable was being tapped. Subjects were then rated for readiness to talk about their own thoughts and feelings (or psychological openness) on the basis of five hours of interviewing. The results showed that the thematic apperception test, the tachistoscopic test, and the inkblot test were correlated with psychological openness (p < .05). What is more, the thematic apperception test proved to be a good predictor of psychological openness eight years later (p < .01).

---

[5] If there is evidence that fantasies and feelings are confused or substituted for reality along with that indicating "openness," the person would, in our nomenclature, be considered "pathologically open."

Levy (1964) played a tape recording in which ten different emotions were expressed vocally. All expressions of emotion were made using the same verbal content. Subjects attempted to identify the various emotions. Subjects' own vocal expressions of the ten feelings were then recorded, again using a single standard paragraph for all emotions. After an intervening two weeks, subjects listened to their own tapes and tried to identify the feelings they had attempted to convey. Finally, judges were presented with the subjects' recordings and asked to assess the emotion being vocalized.

Levy's results indicate that the capacity to identify vocal expressions of emotion is related to the ability to recognize one's own emotional expressions and to communicate emotions to others.

In a similar vein, Mueller and Abeles (1964) found that student counselors whose feelings in counseling. were most accurately judged from tapes were, in turn, the most accurate judges of the feelings of others. These two studies then point to a relationship between the ability to "transmit" and the capacity to understand emotional communications. This bespeaks the importance of the access which a counselor has to his own feelings (psychological openness) to his comprehension of the feelings of others.

Steingart (1962) attempted to connect psychological openness with emotional understanding more directly. Taking his departure from the conception of the understanding process which has been described earlier in the chapter, he hypothesized that subjects who were more tolerant of their feelings and impulses, as gauged from their performances on fingerpainting and dream-telling tests, would be more acute observers in a simulated social situation. His expectations were partially confirmed. Subjects who were able to "give free rein to their thoughts," letting their "dream" stories stray from ordinary description, emerged as superior judges of feelings portrayed in artists' drawings (Steingart, 1962, p. 240).

Goldstein (1961), employing a similar model of interpersonal understanding, had subjects predict the self-ratings of peers on Leary's Interpersonal Check List (ICL) (Laforge and Suczek, 1955). He found that the accuracy of the predictions which subjects made in regard to others' self-ratings on the Love dimension of the ICL was related to the degree of openness which they had in regard to their own feelings in this area. That is, those subjects in whom there was little evidence of a discrepancy between their conscious attitudes (measured by their own responses to the ICL) and their private attitudes (assessed by the TAT) on the Love dimension tended to be the more accurate predictors of the "Love responses" of others than those subjects for whom there were indications of conflict between the two levels.

A comparable study by Mueller (1963) produced similar results. Mueller secured "overt" and "covert" measures of subjects' self-perceptions. The latter was the Activities Index (Stern, 1958), a personality inventory built around Murray's need system (Murray, 1938). The former was a questionnaire drawn from the Activities Index. While the Activities Index asks the subjects to specify their preferences for various activities which the scoring system subsequently converts into indications of need strength, the questionnaire defines each of Murray's constructs directly and asks subjects to rate the applicability of this definition to themselves. Mueller found that the ability of subjects to predict the questionnaire responses of peers was significantly related to their psychological openness, *i.e.*, the degree to which their "overt" ratings agreed with their "covert" ones.

Though the matter is far from settled, there is evidence that psychological openness and the sensitivity to the feelings of others are relatively stable characteristics of individuals. Further, there is a body of empirical data to support theoretical claims that these two characteristics are closely related.

Creation of a Therapeutic Interpersonal Atmosphere

A second major argument for the importance of psychological openness for counselors is that such openness appears to be essential to the establishment of an interpersonal atmosphere that maximally facilitates self-exploration by the client.

Jourard (1964) writes of the "dyadic effect." According to this formulation the extent to which clients are able to reveal themselves to the counselor and, more importantly, to self-recognition is influenced by the openness of the counselor to the client and to himself. In other words, openness begets openness.

Jourard supplies some empirical support for his observation. A group of nursing students was tested on a self-disclosure questionnaire. A year later, they were rated for their ability to "establish and maintain a communicative relationship with patients." Those students who emerged as high self-disclosers received significantly better ratings than those who were low self-disclosers (Jourard, 1958). In another study, subjects exhibited a much greater willingness to reveal themselves to others whom they perceived as being open to them (Jourard, 1959).

Carl Rogers has likewise put heavy emphasis on the "congruence of the counselor" in outlining what he takes to be the "necessary and sufficient conditions" of positive personality change (Rogers, 1957). By "congruence" Rogers refers to the counselor's awareness of his own emotional reactions to the counseling session. That is, in Rogers' words, "the feelings (the counselor) is experiencing are available to him, available to his awareness, and he is able to live these feelings, be them, and able to communicate them if appropriate" (Rogers, 1962, p. 61). It is Rogers' position that unless the counselor possesses this quality in some degree, clients will find it extremely difficult to trust him sufficiently to explore their own experience to the extent required for progress to be made (Rogers, 1962, pp. 61-62). On the other hand, if it is clearly present in the counselor, the client's self-learning will be greatly facilitated (Rogers, 1962, pp. 282-283).

There is some research to support this view. Halkides (1958) took two groups of ten counseling cases from the files of the University of Chicago Counseling

Center. One group was selected as having been "most successful"; the other was seen as "least successful." Random selections of client-counselor interaction were taken from the tape recordings of an early and a later interview in each case. Judges listening to the tape segments rated them for "congruence." Such ratings discriminated successful and nonsuccessful at the .001 level.

Similarly, at the University of Wisconsin, four minute segments were drawn at random from every fifth interview of counseling with 14 different clients. Judges related them for counselor congruence. The results showed that counselors whose clients improved during treatment were rated more congruent than counselors whose clients either did not improve or deteriorated (Truax, 1963).

Butler and Rice (1963) present comparable findings in slightly different terms. They speak of the "expressiveness" of the counselor. They aver that a central task of the counselor is to reintroduce the client to the satisfactions which accompany the generation of fresh new ideas about oneself and one's world and the entertainment of novel experiences. To accomplish this, they hold, the counselor must himself be a person who finds such experiences stimulating rather than one who is separated from them by a stout defensive wall.

Rice's (1965) description points up the degree to which "expressiveness" depends on psychological openness. "Expressive" counselors were identified by the use of metaphorical language, rich in imagery, and by the quality of vocal expressions. The latter was characterized by its high energy (well-harnessed), color, and range—but it was nonetheless undistorted by emotional overflow.

Butler, Rice, and Wagstaff (1962) report that in studies of the course of counseling for 24 clients, those clients treated by the most "expressive" counselors tended to show the most improvement.

Truax and Carkhuff (1965) drew 306 four minute samples from counseling sessions with 16 clients. The extent of each counselor's "transparency" was scored on a five point scale:

(Point #1) (Counselor) is clearly defensive in the interaction and there is explicit evidence of a very considerable discrepancy between his experiencing and his current verbalization. Thus, the (counselor) makes striking contradictions in his statements . . . or, the (counselor) may contradict the content with voice qualities . . .

(Point #5) There is an openness to experience and feelings by the (counselor) of all types—both pleasant and hurtful—without traces of defensiveness or retreat into professionalism (1965, p. 7).

The relationship between the "transparency scale" and client self-exploration, which is shown in the same study to be closely related to adjustment, is significant at the .05 level. An attempt to replicate this study with groups produced a +.79 correlation coefficient between the two variables (p = .05).

Thus, it may be concluded that there is some evidence to confirm the popular notion that the counselor's awareness of his own feelings, his "congruence," or psychological openness, makes an important contribution to the establishment of the type of counseling relationship which is associated with successful outcome.

Summary

This chapter examined the relevance of psychological openness to counseling effectiveness. The hypothesis-generating function of psychological openness in regard to interpersonal understanding was discussed. Empirical findings offered support for the notion (a) that psychological openness is a relatively stable personality variable, (b) that psychological openness is intimately related to the understanding of the feelings of other persons.

Evidence was also presented in support of the hypothesis that the psychological openness of the counselor is an important determinant of the therapeutic atmosphere to be provided for the client.

BIBLIOGRAPHY

Adams, H. F. "The good judge of persons," *Journal of Abnormal and Social Psychology, 22,* 1927, 172-181.

Allen, T. W. "Empathy as a crucial variable in the counseling relationship." Unpublished qualifying paper, Harvard University, 1964.

Allport, G. W. *Personality: A Psychological Interpretation.* New York: Holt, Rinehart and Winston, 1937.

American Psychological Association. *Ethical Standards of Psychologists.* Washington: American Psychological Association, 1953.

American Psychological Association, Committee on Counselor Training. "Recommended standards for training counseling psychologists at the doctoral level," *American Psychologist, 7,* 1952, 175-181.

American Psychological Association, Committee on Training in Clinical Psychology. "Recommended graduate training program in clinical psychology," *American Psychologist, 2,* 1947, 539-558.

Bakan, D. "Clinical psychology and logic," *The American Psychologist, 11,* 1956, 655-662.

Barron, F. *Creativity and Psychological Health.* Princeton, New Jersey: D. Van Nostrand Co., Inc., 1963.

Blum, G. S. *The Blacky Pictures.* New York: Psychological Corporation, 1950.

Blum, G. S. "Perceptual defense revisited," in *Research in Personality*, eds. Martha T. Mednick and Sarnoff A. Mednick, New York: Holt, Rinehart and Winston, 1963, 147-155.

Bordin, E. S. *Psychological Counseling.* New York: Appleton-Century-Crofts, 1955.

Brofenbrenner, U., J. Harding, and M. Gallway. "The measurement of skill in social perception," in *Talent and Society*, eds. D. McClelland, A. Baldwin, U. Brofenbrenner, and F. Strodbeck, Princeton, New Jersey: D. Van Nostrand Co., Inc., 1958, 29-108.

Bruner, J. "The conditions of creativity," in *Contemporary Approaches to Creative Thinking*, eds. H. E. Gruber, G. Tenell, and M. Wertheimer, New York: Atherton, 1962, 1-30.

Bruner, J., and R. Tagiuri "The perception of people," in *Handbook of Social Psychology*, 2 ed. C. Lindzey, Cambridge, Mass.: Addison-Wesley, 1954, 634-654.

Butler, J. N., and L. N. Rice, "Adience, self-actualization, and drive theory," in *Concepts of Personality*, eds. J. M. Wepman and R. W. Heine, London: Methuen, 1963, 79-112.

Butler, M. M., L. N. Rice, and A. K. Wagstaff. "On the Naturalistic definitions of variables," on *Research in Psychotherapy*. II, eds. H. H. Strupp and L. Luborsky, Washington: American Psychological Association. 1962, 178-205.

Butler, M. M., L. N. Rice, and A. K. Wagstaff. "Process affecting scores on 'understanding of others' and 'assumed similarity,' " *Psychological Bulletin*, 52, 1955, 177-194.

Cutler, R. L. "Countertransference effects in psychotherapy," *Journal of Consulting Psychology*, 22, 1958, 349-356.

Dellis, N. P. "Discussion," in *The Training of Psychotherapists: A Multi-disciplinary Approach*, eds. N. P. Dellis and H. K. Stone, Baton Rouge: University of Louisiana, 1960, 43-46.

Dollard, J., and N. Miller. *Personality and Psychotherapy.* New York; McGraw-Hill, 1950.

Dymond, R. F. "A preliminary investigation of the relation of insight and empathy," *Journal of Consulting Psychology*, 12, 1948, 228-233.

Ellsworth, S. "The consistency of counselor feeling-verbalization in and outside of the counselor-client relationship." Unpublished doctoral dissertation, Michigan State University, 1962.

Ellsworth, S. "The consistency of counselor feeling-verbalization," *Journal of Counseling Psychology*, 10, 1963, 356-361.

Emlaw, R., R. Mosher, N. Sprinthall, and J. Whiteley. "Teacher effectiveness: A method for prediction and evaluation," *The National Elementary Principal*, 43, 1963, 38-49.

Feder, D. S. "The training and role of a counselor," *SRA Guidance Newsletter*, 1, March, 1961.

Fenichel, O. *The Psychoanalytic Theory of Neurosis.* New York: Norton, 1945.

Fliess, R. "The metapsychology of the analyst," *Psychoanalytic Quarterly, 11,* 1942, 211-226.

Frenkel-Brunswick, E. "Motivation and behavior," *Genetic Psychological Monograph, 26,* 1942, 121-265.

Freud, S. *The Standard Edition of the Complete Psychological Works of Sigmund Freud.* London: The Hogarth Press, 1957.

Getzels, J., and P. Jackson. *Creativity and Intelligence.* New York: Wiley, 1962.

Goldstein, L. "Empathy and its relationship to personality factors and personality organization." Unpublished doctoral dissertation, New York University, 1961.

Green, G. H. "Insight and group adjustment," *Journal of Abnormal and Social Psychology, 43,* 1948, 49-61.

Greenson, R. R. "Empathy and its vicissitudes," *International Journal of Psychoanalysis, 41,* 1961, 418-424.

Halkides, G. "An experimental study of four conditions necessary for therapeutic change." Unpublished doctoral dissertation, University of Chicago, 1958.

Hartmann, H. *Ego Psychology and the Problem of Adaptation* (trans. by D. Rapaport). New York: International Universities Press, 1958.

Jones, E. *The Life and Work of Sigmund Freud.* II. New York: Basic Books, 1955.

Jourard, S. M. "Self-disclosure and grades in nursing college," *Journal of Applied Psychology, 56,* 1958, 91-98.

Jourard, S. M. "Self-disclosure and other cathexis," *Journal of Abnormal and Social Psychology, 59,* 1959, 428-431.

Jourard, S. M. *The Transparent Self.* New York: D. Van Nostrand Co., Inc., 1964.

Kagan, J. "Stylistic variables in fantasy behavior: The ascription of affect states to social stimuli," in *Contemporary Issues in Thematic Apperceptive Methods,* Springfield, Illinois: Charles C. Thomas, 1961, 196-220.

Kagan, J., and G. Lesser (eds.). *Contemporary Issues in Thematic Apperceptive Methods.* Springfield, Illinois: Charles C. Thomas, 1961.

Kaplan, A. *The Conduct of Inquiry.* San Francisco: Chandler, 1964.

Katz, R. L. *Empathy: Its Nature and Uses.* New York: Free Press of Glencoe, 1963.

Kelly, G. A. *The Psychology of Personal Constructs.* New York: Norton, 1955.

Knight, R. P. "The present status of organized pscyhoanalysis in the United States," *American Journal of Psychoanalysis, 1,* 1953, 197.

Kubie, L. S. *Neurotic Distortion of the Creative Process.* Lawrence, Kansas: University of Kansas Press, 1958.

Laforge, R., and R. Suczek. "The interpersonal dimension of personality: III. An interpersonal check list," *Journal of Personality, 24,* 1955, 94-112.

Lemann, T. B., and R. L. Solomon. "Group characteristics as revealed in sociometric patterns and personality ratings," *Sociometry, 15,* 1952, 7-90.

Levy, P. K. "The ability to express and perceive vocal communications of feeling," in *The Communication of Emotional Meaning,* ed. J. R. Davitz, New York: McGraw-Hill, 1964, 43-55.

Lief, H. I. "Training in broad spectrum psychotherapy," in *The Training of Psychotherapists: A Multidisciplinary Approach*, eds., N. P. Dellis and H. K. Stone, Baton Rouge: University of Louisiana, 1960, 68-81.

Lubin, B. "Note," *American Psychologist*, 20, 1965, 236-237.

Maslow, A. "Creativity in self-actualizing people," in *Creativity and its Cultivation*, ed. H. Anderson, New York: Harper and Row, 1959, 83-95.

McArthur, C. "Analyzing the clinical process," *Journal of Counseling Psychology*, 1, 1954, 203-207.

McArthur, C. "The dynamic model," *Journal of Counseling Psychology*, 3, 1956, 168-171.

Meehl, P. E. *Clinical Versus Statistical Prediction*. Minneapolis: University of Minnesota, 1954.

Menninger, K., M. Mayman, and Paul Pruyser. *The Vital Balance*. New York: Viking, 1963.

Mueller, W. J., and N. Abeles. "The components of empathy and their relationship to the projection on human movement responses," *Journal of Projective Technology*, 28, 1964, 322-330.

Murray, H. A. "The effect of fear upon estimates of the maliciousness of other personalities," *Journal of Social Psychology*, 4, 1933, 310-329.

Murray, H. A. *Explorations in Personality*. London: Oxford, 1938.

Posner, B. A. "Selfishness, guilt feelings, and social distance." Unpublished Masters' Thesis, University of Iowa, 1940.

Postman, L. "On the problem of perceptual defense," *Psychological Review*, 60, 1953, 298-306.

Putnam, J. J. *On Freud's Psychoanalytic Method and Its Evaluation*. Philadelphia: Lippincott, 1912.

Rapaport, D., R. Schafer, and N. Gill. *Diagnostic Psychological Testing*, II. Chicago: World Book, 1946.

Rice, L. "Therapist's style of participation and case outcome," *Journal of Consulting Psychology*, 29, 1965, 155-160.

Rogers, C. R. *Client-Centered Therapy*. Boston: Houghton Mifflin, 1951.

Rogers, C. R. *Counseling and Psychotherapy*. Boston: Houghton Mifflin, 1942.

Rogers, C. R. "The interpersonal relationship: The core of guidance," *Harvard Educational Review*, 32, 1962, 416-429.

Rogers, C. R. "Necessary and sufficient conditions of therapeutic personality change." *Journal of Consulting Psychology*, 21, 1957, 95-103.

Rogers, C. R. *On Becoming a Person*. Boston: Houghton-Mifflin, 1961.

Rokeach, M. *The Open and Closed Mind*. New York: Basic Books, 1960.

Rokeach, M. "Studies in beauty: II. Some determiners of the perception of beauty in woman," *Journal of Social Psychology*, 22, 1945, 155-169.

Sarbin, T. R., R. Taft, and D. E. Bailey. *Clinical Inference and Cognitive Theory*. New York: Holt, Rinehart and Winston, 1960.

Schachtel, E. *Metamorphosis: On the Development of Affect, Perception, Attention, and Memory*. New York: Basic Books, 1959.

Schafer, R. "Generative empathy in the treatment situation," *Psychoanalytic Quarterly*, 28, 1959, 342-373.

Sears, R. R. "Experimental studies of projection: I. Attribution of traits," *Journal of Social Psychology,* 7, 1936, 151-168.

Solley, C. M., and G. Murphy. *Development of the Perceptual World.* New York: Basic Books, 1960.

Sprinthall, N. A., J. M. Whiteley, and R. L. Mosher. "Study of teacher effectiveness," *Journal of Teacher Education,* 18, 1966, 93-106 (a).

Sprinthall, N. A., J. M. Whiteley, and R. L. Mosher. "Cognitive flexibility as a dimension of counselor behavior. Definition, rationale, research focus," *Counselor Education and Supervision,* 5, 1966, 188-197 (b).

Steingart, I. "Conditions of personality organization related to empathetic ability among normal and schizophrenic adults," *Journal of Consulting Psychology,* 26, 1962, 416-421.

Stern, G. *Activities Index: Preliminary Manual.* Syracuse: Psychological Research Center, Syracuse University, 1958.

Striber, F. D. "Self-concept factors affecting the judgments of others." Unpublished Doctoral Dissertation, University of Nebraska, *Dissertation Abstract,* 1961, 3858.

Striber, F. D. *Psychotherapists in Action.* New York: Grune and Stratton, 1960.

Taft, R. "Some correlates of the ability to make accurate social judgments." Unpublished Doctoral Dissertation, University of California, 1950.

Tagiuri, R., and L. Petrullo (eds.). *Person Perception and Interpersonal Behavior.* Stanford, California: Stanford University Press, 1958.

Truax, C. B. "Effective ingredients in psychotherapy: An approach to unraveling the patient-therapist interaction," *Journal of Counseling Psychology,* 10, 1963, 25-263.

Truax, C. B. "A scale for the measurement of accurate empathy," *Discussion Paper,* No. 20. Madison, Wisconsin: Psychiatric Institute, University of Wisconsin, 1961.

Truax, C. B., and R. R. Carkhuff. "Client and therapist transparency in the psychotherapeutic encounter," *Journal of Counseling Psychology,* 12, 1965, 3-9.

Tyler, L. E. *The Work of the Counselor.* 2nd ed. New York: Appleton-Century-Crofts, 1961.

Weigart, E. "The nature of sympathy in the art of psychotherapy," *Psychiatry,* 24, 1961, 187-196.

Weitz, H. "Counseling as a function of the counselor's personality," *Personnel and Guidance Journal,* 35, 1957, 276-280.

Whiteley, J., N. Sprinthall, R. Mosher, and R. Donaghy. "Selection and evaluation of counselor effectiveness," *Journal of Counseling Psychology,* 14, 1967, 226-234.

6

Psychological Openness and Counselor Effectiveness: A Pilot Study

It appears that psychological openness is a concept of considerable promise in regard to the knotty problem of predicting the effectiveness of counselors. The present chapter describes a study designed to test the hypothesis that the effectiveness of the counseling performed by students in an introductory counseling practicum will be directly related to the degree of psychological openness characteristic of them.

The Operational Definitions

The Independent Variable: Psychological Openness

Psychological openness has been defined as the capacity of a person to use his feelings, impulses, and fantasies for adaptive purposes. In considering how this construct might best be measured, attention to projective techniques. As Sundberg's survey (1961) revealed, these instruments are the most commonly employed methods of personality assessment. On the other hand, as Kerlinger writes, "projective measures are probably the most controversial of psychological measurement instruments" (1964, p. 557). After a great deal of somewhat uncritical enthusiasm, they have recently subjected to much strong criticism, e.g., Eysenck (1955), Super (1959), Berg and Adams (1962).[1]

However, regardless of the value one puts on projective techniques in general, it should not be overlooked that some promising results have been obtained with them in regard to "openness." Let us examine these findings.

As mentioned above, Kagan (1961) found that subjects who responded to an inkblot test and to a thematic apperception test in terms of feelings were more

---

1 It should be noted that even the most unrelenting critics of projective techniques seem at the same time to be intrigued by their possibilities. The brunt of the attacks has therefore been borne by the current orthodoxy in regard to the interpretation of the data and not so much by the potentialities of techniques as data gathering devices.

willing to discuss their own motives and emotions with an interviewer than those whose responses contained very little reference to affect. Tutko (1962) hypothesized that people who were strongly motivated for approval would be less open to their socially undesirable thoughts and feelings than those whose need for approval was more moderate. Congruent with his hypothesis, his data revealed that there was a significant inverse relationship between "revealingness" on the Thematic Apperception Test, the Rorschach, and the Incomplete Sentences Blank and the "need for approval" on the Marlowe-Crowne Social Desirability Scale (Marlowe and Crowne, 1964).

Masling's (1961) review of the experimental data suggests that differences in number and type of Rorschach responses are related to the readiness of subjects to communicate information about themselves. Desroches and Larsen (1964) divided their subjects into three groups according to the guardedness of their behavior. They found that the groups could be ordered along this dimension by means of six Rorschach variables ($p < .00002$).

Thus, it is suggested that the willingness of persons to recognize their subjective reactions can be assessed from certain projective techniques with some confidence. However, some doubt adheres to these results because of the moderate level of interscorer reliability (as in Tutko) or because of the lack of any data on the matter (as in the other studies cited). Nor, save for Kagan (1961), is any reliability information available. Clearly what is required is an attempt to capitalize on the richness of the projective data which is somewhat more satisfactory from the standpoint of conventional psychometrics.

One possible measure which meets these conditions is the Rorschach Index of Repressive Style (RIRS) (Levine and Spivack, 1964).

Rorschach Index of Repressive Style

The RIRS utilizes data gathered from the standard administration of the Rorschach. Schafer (1954), for one, has made the point that in order to respond to projective techniques, especially to the Rorschach, with responses which exceed simple descriptions and banalities the subject must have recourse to the less objective, more feeling-directed aspects of his experience, to fantasy. The nature of the task the Rorschach poses is such that the subject must give himself over to the more whimsical, less reality-bound aspects of his experience or be content with brief, bland, stereotyped productions. Thus, in this theoretical context, a subject's departure from blandness and stereotypy in his Rorschach responses provides an index of the degree to which he can use the less-formalized, more feeling-laden thought processes. It is, in other words, a potentially useful indicator of psychological openness. Indeed, it was upon this insight that the studies in the foregoing section were predicted.

The importance of the RIRS is that it is a relatively objective system for the assessment of the extent to which a subject departs from vagueness and banality. The more a subject responds in terms of indefinite, obvious percepts, the lower his RIRS score. The more specific and elaborate his responses, the more they show evidences of fantasy or feeling, the more credit he receives on the RIRS scale.

A somewhat different line of reasoning furnishes what is, perhaps, an even more convincing case for the RIRS as a measure of openness. Taking the lead from Hartshorne and May (1928), from Edwards (1957), and Marlowe and Crowne (1964), attention may be turned to the "response set" or "response style" of the subjects. In this case, the subtle psychodynamics of the Rorschach response can be ignored. That is, speculation concerning the alleged contribution of the "preconscious" and the "unconscious" may be abandoned. Rather, the belief of all subjects in a sample in the efficacy of the Rorschach test as a probe of their inner lives may serve as the point of departure. Believing themselves to be under scrutiny by a sort of psychological X-ray, it may be supposed that some subjects will anxiously seek concealment. They will play it "close to the vest," as it were, giving vague, noncommittal, socially circumspect responses—as if to give the tester little "to get his teeth into" (Levine and Spivack, 1964, p. 19). Other subjects unburdened by such reticence concerning self-disclosure may be expected to indulge themselves in the free play of fantasy which the test instructions seek to promote.

It would seem that one is on relatively firm ground in attributing greater "openness" to these subjects as compared with the former—regardless of the actual predictive power of standard Rorschach interpretation. When viewed from this perspective, the RIRS assumes considerable importance. It is designed to discriminate between these two groups. The question of the Rorschach's capacity to determine the values of significant personality variables may be put aside. Attention is shifted from the "meaning" of responses in the conventional sense to the degree of specification and elaboration, the amount of departure from the commonplace typical of them. These may be considered to be indices of the *willingness* and/or *capability* to risk a revelation of himself.

Again, the concern is not with such questions as what personal material does a subject allow to emerge, for example, is the response "a grotesque witch" revelatory of the subject's attitude toward his mother? Rather the point of interest is, do the responses of the subject indicate that he is able to risk the emergence of such material? Apprised of the object of the Rorschach, to reveal the nature of his inner life, can he permit himself to "play the game," to respond freely— elaborating, specifying, letting his imagination have free rein? Those who are able to do so are deemed "open"; those who are not, "closed."

Following either line of reasoning (the "psychodynamic" or the "response set" line), then, the RIRS appears to be of substantial relevance to the assessment of psychological openness. Several studies are available to support this conclusion.

Research Summary: The succeeding studies provide empirical support for the notion developed above, that the RIRS is a promising measure of psychological openness. If one assumes that the RIRS reflects the extent to which a person is able to use inner experiences for adaptation, one would expect that persons with high RIRS scores would respond better to a situation which throws them back on such experiences than those with low RIRS scores. Accordingly, Holt and Goldberger (1959) administered the Rorschach to subjects and placed them in a sensory deprivation situation. The experimental conditions reduced the external stimulation they received to an absolute minimum and the focus was placed directly on that from internal sources. Two reaction patterns were identified from tapes of the subjects' verbalization during their isolation: one, labeled "adaptive," involved cooperation and enjoyment of one's own imagery; the other, orthogonal to the first, was labeled "maladaptive" and was characterized by discomfort and complaints.

True to expectation those subjects with high RIRS scores adapted best to the situation, freely enjoying their thoughts and feelings. [2] In striking contrast, the low RIRS subjects tended to be unable or unwilling to utilize their thoughts and feelings to adapt. Indeed, they tended to find them disturbing in themselves (Holt and Goldberger, 1959; Spivack and Levine, 1964, pp. 91ff).

Further confirmation comes from studies of "field dependence" (Witkin et al., 1954). These involve several perceptual tests designed to determine the extent to which subjects can ignore deceptive external stimulation in favor of more veridical internal cues. Those subjects who cannot do so are called "field dependent"; those who can, "field independent." They seem to represent broad personality types. As Levine and Spivack note:

> Witkin's studies of field dependence have suggested that field dependent subjects are characterized by a lack of awareness of inner life, a fear of aggressive and sexual impulses and poor control of these impulses. Field independent subjects have greater awareness of inner life and a great effectiveness of discharge control of these impulses (1964, p. 93).

Since one of the differences between the two groups (field independent and field dependent) seems to be a discrepancy in terms of psychological openness, one might expect some relationship to obtain between field dependence and the RIRS. The scores of 92 college students on the three field dependence tests (Rod and Frame Test, Embedded Figures, Chair-Window) were compared with their RIRS. Since subjects were divided according to sex, there were six correlations. Of the six, all were negative in direction, as predicted. Two reached the .05 level of significance and two others fell short of it by a single correlation point (Spivack and Levine, 1964, p. 94). Thus, as the RIRS increased, there was a tendency for subjects to demonstrate a capacity to use internal cues. Or, looking at the matter somewhat differently, higher RIRS scores tended to appear among subjects who were characterized in terms similar to psychological openness (field independence) on other tasks.

---

2 The RIRS correlated $+.61$ (rho; $p =$ less than .05) with the adaptive syndrome and $+.73$ (rho $p = .01$) with the richness of the imagery produced during isolation (Holt and Goldberger, 1959).

Gardner *et al.* (1959) set their subjects a different perceptual task. Subjects were asked to judge the relative size of a series of closely matched squares. It was hypothesized that those subjects who were more "open" to their experience, who did not use repression extensively, would be superior judges. In part, the rationale for such a hypothesis was that successful judgments would require the retention of earlier squares in the mind. This would be difficult for "repressors," people who use repression extensively, because they may be supposed to let one memory fuse readily with another as part of their normal mental functioning. Gardner *et al.* (1959) and Holzman and Gardner (1959) lend credence to this notion. The poor judges were indeed found to be "repressors"; the good judges, on the other hand, emerged as persons much more open to their internal promptings.

One would expect, then, that good judges would score higher on the RIRS if this measure is indeed related to openness. For the 20 subjects that Gardner *et al.* (1959) employed, the RIRS was found to be directly related to ranking accuracy (rho = $+.44$; p = .03) (Levine and Spivack, 1964, p. 97).

It would seem, therefore, that there is a reasonable body of findings which are congruent with the claim that the RIRS is meaningfully related to the construct "psychological openness." That is, in the studies cited, as one moves up the RIRS scale, one finds a tendency toward greater awareness of and tolerance for thoughts, feelings, and impulses which may stray off the path of conventionality and acceptability. The higher the RIRS, the greater the probability that a subject will be able to use such material adaptively. This is, of course, the definition of psychological openness.

Corrected RIRS

It appears, however, that the RIRS procedure described above is ill-suited to discriminate what might be termed "pseudo-open" subjects from those who are psychologically open in the main sense of the term. It is conceivable that in a given case maladaptive responses might be mistaken for openness. A subject's departure from banal, commonplace responses may betoken an impairment of his capacity to evaluate the appropriateness of possible responses and/or to inhibit those which are inappropriate. Or, again, it might be indicative of a deviant response set. In other words, an elevated RIRS score may be the product of poorly controlled impulses and feelings or of an aberrant response style, as well as of the ability to participate freely in the task, giving imagination free rein without grave doubts concerning self-exposure. This possibility has been dealt with at some length by Holt (1960) and Silverman (1965).

Holt has proposed a set of criteria by which adaptive openness may be distinguished from its maladaptive counterpart:

> "Form level": In general, adaptive responses are plausible interpretations of the aspects of the blots to which they have reference.

"Control categories": Though a subject may occasionally give a response that may be considered to be bizarre, it is almost inevitably justified in terms of the objective world. For instance, the response, "a woman with snakes coming out of her head," suggests maladaptation. The response, "Medusa," on the other hand, justifies the basic percept sufficiently to suggest psychological openness by giving it a more appropriate context (Silverman, 1965, p. 239). Presumably the very minimum of control would involve an awareness of the peculiarity of his responses.

"Affect accompaniment": The open subject may well derive some pleasure from his efforts; at very least, it is to be expected that he will not be seriously threatened by the Rorschach. Conversely the speciously open subject can be expected to be uneasy with the task—either in terms of the material that he has produced, the meaning it has for him, or the implications he feels it may have.

While all three of these criteria are relevant to the evaluation of the subjects at hand, Holt's "affect accompaniment" has been chosen for investigation. Holt suggests that it be assessed from the subject's "expressive behavior" during the test. The question is: Are there any marked behavioral indications that the subject is greatly threatened by the task? Such indications, blatant hostility toward the tester and/or the test; physical manifestations of distress, such as excessive sighing, blanching, trembling, inappropriate posturing; repeated attempts to assure oneself of the impotence of the test, are to be taken as evidence of a lack of psychological openness, the RIRS score notwithstanding.

This conclusion appears creditable when viewed in the "response set" frame of reference as well. The behavior which would be, in Holt's psychodynamic frame, attributed to anxiety vis-à-vis images from "unconscious" and "preconscious" sources, is here laid to stout opposition to the self-revelation the test promises. In either case, it seems incompatible with openness.

To utilize Holt's correction for "affect accompaniment" in regard to the RIRS, it is necessary to turn to the observations of the Rorschach testers involved. Unfortunately, in the study to be reported below, since there was only a single tester for each subject, there can be no quantitative estimate of observer reliability. What can be done, however, is to have the tester specify the nature of the observations which suggest that a subject is relatively deficient in adaptive openness. The exploratory nature of the present research would seem to justify such a procedure.

Therefore, subjects might be ordered according to RIRS with the exception that those subjects judged to be greatly threatened by the test would be given the lowest ranks for psychological openness regardless of their RIRS scores. This ordering would be referred to as the "Corrected RIRS."

Group Supervision Reports

One of the most important aspects of the introductory practicum in counseling at the Harvard Graduate School of Education (HGSE) is the group supervision that is provided. Students meet each week with their university supervisors in small groups of six. These meetings, approximately one and a half hours in duration, are dedicated to the discussion of tape recordings of group members' counseling. Each subject presents material for discussion on at least one occasion. After presenting at the particular session concerned with his work, each subject is to write up his "reactions" to the session.

Of course, only the smallest fraction of the material of the group session can be reported within the scope of the students' reports. Since the principle of selection is the province of the student, the reports seem to be potentially rich sources of information about the subject as a counselor.

This supposition is strengthened by Ellsworth's findings (1963). The data suggest that there is an appreciable degree of consistency between the manner in which a subject responds to a group supervision session and his style of counseling.

Secondly, as Allport (1942) has shown, documents of this kind are indeed profitable sources of information concerning the personality of the writer. Thus, given the assumption that "openness" is an important and pervasive personality characteristic, it might be expected to be evident, to some degree, in the students' reports.

For instance, it might be predicted that the most "closed" students would deal mainly with external matters, restricting themselves to factual accounts of sessions. They might be expected to avoid evaluations of their own work and/or to limit evaluation to the faults of others in the group.

Those students who were slightly more open might be more inclined to acknowledge the critical comments of others, but be unable to give any indication of their feelings in regard to them.

The next level of openness would be occupied by students who comment on their own shortcomings as counselors or who pick up suggestions by group members and draw out their implications.

On a still higher level would be those students who comment on their own feelings in regard to the counseling session itself or to evaluations of counseling by the group, by a supervisor, or selves—albeit quite briefly and without elaboration.

Finally, students whose own feelings and attitudes are the central themes of their reports might be supposed to be the most "open."

Accordingly, it might be expected that a scale built on these principles would be useful in the assessment of "openness" from the reports of group supervision. Therefore, a scale—the Group Supervision Report Scale, or GSRS—was constructed by the writer. It is presented in Appendix C.

The Dependent Variable: Effectiveness in Counseling

In the foregoing section, two possible measures of psychological openness have been suggested. Attention must now be turned to the operational definition of "the effectiveness of counseling."

Supervisor Ratings

The problem of assessing the level of performance of counselors has proved to be a perplexing one. The solution appears to be obvious. One must simply measure the progress of clients. However, as Kelly and Fiske (1951), Holt and Luborsky (1958) and Sprinthall, Whiteley, and Mosher (1965) confess, such "ultimate" criteria are not readily available. Despite the magnitude of the studies in which each group of authors was involved, no progress was made in developing such criteria. Rather, all of these investigators have utilized the ratings of supervisors. It may, of course, be argued that, in fact, the careers of students in counseling depend almost wholly upon judgments of this sort.

Patently, the determination of the validity of such judgments is a matter which urgently requires empirical investigation. However, it is clear that supervisors are generally in possession of a good deal of information relevant to the judgment task. In the present instance, sources of information available to supervisors included tapes of each student's counseling, his participation in the group seminar, his notes of counseling sessions, the comments of his supervisors in his placement setting, and his response to group and individual supervision.

Although the burden of processing this welter of information falls heavily on the supervisors' subjective frames of reference, there is some evidence of consistency among individual supervisors. First, there are suggestions that there is considerable agreement among supervisors in regard to the basic dimensions of counselor behavior crucial to successful practice. For example, Holt and Luborsky (1958) report that supervisors' judgments of the psychotherapeutic competence of their psychiatric residents showed appreciable interrater reliability and were stable across time. Further, the well-known research of Fiedler (1950a, 1950b) indicates that experienced counselors of divergent theoretical orientations can reach high levels of agreement concerning the most important characteristics of the basic counseling relationship. Finally, an unpublished study of the opinions of supervisors concerned with the Master's program in guidance at the Harvard Graduate School of Education suggests that considerable agreement exists among them in regard to the nature of the behaviors characteristic of the "good counselor" (Broudy et al., 1964).

Kelly and Fiske (1951) had three judges from each university participating in the study of the assessment of trainees in clinical psychology, and three judges from practicum placement rate their trainees for clinical competence. The medium level of agreement for university judges was +.74, for practicum judges, +.73.

More direct evidence of the usefulness of supervisor ratings is provided by Abeles (1958). In his follow-up study of 130 counselors trained at the University of Texas, Abeles found that the ratings of supervisors were valid as well as reliable predictors of the level of success in counseling attained two years after graduation.

Thus, while it is clear that further work is required to establish the precise value of any given set of supervisor judgments, the great reliance placed upon them by training institutions and the sketchy data at hand dictate their use as a measure of counselor effectiveness.

Measurement: In order to maximize the reliability and the validity of supervisor judgments, it is necessary to reduce the ambiguity of the judgment task. To accomplish this, two moderately structured scales were developed. The first is a seven-point scale of "overall clinical competence" running from "extremely effective: works well with clients; approaches 'ideal,' " at one extreme, to "negative effectiveness: doesn't really listen or understand clients; preoccupied with himself or irrelevancies," at the other (Appendix B). The scale was a product of the discussion by all of the supervisors who used it. All agreed that it was reasonably clear and meaningful.

The second was an eleven-point Q-sort (Stephenson, 1953) developed by the author. Thirty-eight items were to be sorted into a quasi-normal distribution to describe the counseling behavior of each subject. The majority of the items were drawn from a pool of items presented by Fiedler (1950*a*). The Fiedler items have reference to behavior of demonstrated relevance to counseling. Thirty items of the present set were selected so as to represent all of the dimensions of the Fiedler deck. However, an attempt was made to reduce the apparent redundancies it contains. The remaining nine items were supplied by the investigator. These items are parallel to the categories of a rating scheme employed to rate subjects' responses to a quasi-counseling situation (to be outlined in the next section). Definitions and examples were provided for some of the more complex or ambiguous items.

Subjects' scores were derived from the Q-sorts by means of reference to items 6, 12, 18, 21 [3] . These items deal explicitly with subjects' responsiveness to client feeling. The importance of such responsiveness will be dealt with in the next section. Greatest weight was given to the item concerned with the counselor's response to client feelings which are implied but not explicitly stated. Responses which organized several client expressions of feeling were weighted next most heavily. Responses which conveyed simple recognition of client feeling were given less weight and questions concerning client feeling were given least weight.

Therefore, two measures of effectiveness in counseling were derived from supervisors' judgments. The first calls for a global assessment of competence on a seven-point scale. The second requires a specification of the degree to which subjects tend to respond to the feelings of clients in counseling.

---

3   Q-sort items
  6. Responds to client feelings beyond those explicitly verbalized by the client.
  12. Reorganizes client expressions of feeling so as to clarify them.
  18. Turns client attention to feelings by means of questions.
  21. Acknowledges client's explicit feelings.

Responses to a Simulated Counseling Interview

Experimental Conditions

Although supervisors' judgments cannot be ignored as criteria for counselor performance, they require suppletion. Ideally, the supplementary method should facilitate the comparison of subjects and allow for the determination of interobserver agreement.

The former requirement is derived from the fact that one apparent score of error in the supervisory ratings is the wide variety of experiences provided by the introductory practicum in counseling at Harvard. That is, some students are placed in elementary schools, others in high schools, vocational schools, or colleges. In addition, some students are assigned particularly difficult clients; others see only untroubled clients for routine matters. To complicate the situation further, some placement agencies accept sound tape recordings of interviews more readily than others. Therefore, there clearly exists a need for a measure which brings the differences among students into bolder relief.

Such a technique is suggested by Strupp (1960). Subjects are presented with a sound motion picture of an actual counseling interview. The film is stopped in 28 predetermined places and the subjects were allowed 30 seconds in each case to write down the response they would make were they the counselor. This procedure yields comparable samples of quasi-counseling behavior which may be rated by independent observers whose agreement can be specified quantitatively.

Responsiveness to Client Affect Scales (RCAS)

A rating scale to be applied to the response of subjects to the film has been developed by the investigator (Allen, 1966). It is, at base, a method for the content analysis of counselor verbalizations which takes its departure from that suggested by Snyder (1947). Counselor statements are sorted into any of the 17 categories according to specified rules. The categories are given in Table 8.

Once the individual counselor statements have been categorized, the number of responses to "feelings" made by each respondent is ascertained. Subjects are then ranked according to these scores. The highest score is given rank one; the next highest score is given rank two. This ranking will be known herein as the Response to Client Affect Scale Score or the RCAS.

The justification for such a procedure, that of placing the greatest weight on "response to feeling" at the expense of other factors, rests, in part, on the unanimity of writers from a wide variety of schools of thought in counseling in regard to its importance (Rogers, 1942, 1944, 1951; Fiedler, 1950a, 1950b; Frank, 1962; Wolberg, 1954; Bordin, 1955).

More persuasive is the growing body of research support for the notion that responses to feeling are related to successful counseling. Kirtner and Cartwright

(1959) found positive outcome in 42 counseling cases to be related to the degree to which clients were able to talk about their own feelings in counseling. From this it may be inferred that counselor activity directed toward such client behavior is important to progress in counseling. However, caution must be exercised in the interpretation of these results. It should be noted that the outcome measure employed consisted of therapist judgments made on a nine-point scale. Given the

TABLE 8

Scoring Categories of the Responsiveness to Client Affect Scale [4]

Acceptance [a]
Approval [b]
Non-Directive Lead [b]
Reassurance [b]
Structuring
Silence

RESPONSE TO FEELING

Questions about client feeling
Acknowledgment of feelings explicitly mentioned by the client
Reorganizing client expressions of feeling
Responses to feelings not specifically verbalized

INTERPRETATION

Questions intended to turn the client's attention to the causes of his experience. Suggestions to the client of connections among various aspects of his experience. [a]

RESPONSES TO CONTENT

Factual questions
Restatement of a client's idea/repetition of client statement [b]
Information [b]
Evaluation advice [c]

Miscellaneous

---

4 Cf. Allen (1966) for scoring manual and a description of the scoring categories noted above
a Category and description taken from Snyder (1947, pp. 333-336).
b Category and description: a modification of Snyder (1947, pp. 333-336).
c Category and description: a modification of Porter (1950, p. 201).

client-centered bias that the ability to discuss one's own feelings is an indication of personal adjustment, (Rogers 1961), it might be supposed that a client who expressed his feelings freely in counseling would receive a higher outcome rating by that fact alone.

Snyder (1945) took a somewhat different approach. He found in his study of the counseling process that there was a "marked tendency" of clients to participate in the counseling interview after feeling responses by the counselor. Bergman (1951) investigated the nature of the client behavior which followed the various classes of counselor verbalization. He reports that,

> Reflection of feeling is the only counselor response which is followed more often by continued self-exploration or insight than would be expected by chance alone. The deviation is significant at the 1 per cent level. This counselor response is the only one which is followed less often by abandonment of self-exploration than would be expected by chance. The deviation is significant at the .01 per cent level (Bergman, 1951, p. 233).

Similarly, Speisman (1959) found that counselor statements of "medium depth" were positively related to client self-exploration and negatively to "resistance." Other classes of response, those more "superficial" and those of more "depth," were unrelated to self-exploration and positively related to resistance. "Superficial responses" resemble the "content responses" in the foregoing scoring system: "deep level responses" are equivalent to "interpretations," and "medium level responses" closely approximate the categories "reorganization of feeling" and "response to implicit feeling" in the present study. Frank and Sweetland (1962) analyzed the first four interviews of four counselors with 40 clients. They found that responses to feeling were followed by "increased understanding" and "insight" responses on the part of the client at two and three times chance expectancy. Finally, Rottschafer and Renjaglia (1962) report that feeling responses evoke less dependent client behavior than other classes of counselor verbalization.

Thus, preliminary investigations offer support for the theoretical notion that the tendency to respond to the feelings of clients is an important aspect of counselor behavior. It would seem therefore that it is one reasonable criterion of the effectiveness of students in counseling.

Experimental Predictions

The general hypothesis for this investigation is that the effectiveness of the counseling of students in an introductory practicum in guidance will be directly related to psychological openness. In the preceding sections, operational definitions have been suggested for the principle terms of the hypothesis. That is, it has been argued that the Corrected Rorschach Index of Repressive Style and the amount of feeling expressed in reports of case presentations in group supervision are appropriate measures of psychological openness. Further, a case has been made that supervisor judgments of overall competence and estimates of responsiveness to client feeling from supervisor judgments and from responses to a simulated counseling situation are acceptable "proximate" measures of counseling effectiveness. Consequently, the strength of the general hypothesis may be tested by means of the following predictions.

Prediction 1:   Supervisor ratings of students in an introductory practicum in counseling for overall competence in counseling will be directly related to the Corrected Rorschach Index of Repressive Style.

Prediction 2:   Supervisor Q-sort ratings of students' responsiveness to client feelings will be directly related to the Corrected Rorschach Index of Repressive Style.

Prediction 3:   The responsiveness of students to the feelings of a client in a filmed counseling interview will be directly related to the Corrected Rorschach Index of Repressive Style.

Prediction 4:   Supervisor ratings of students for overall competence in counseling will be directly related to the degree to which personal feelings are expressed in reports of group supervision.

Prediction 5:   Supervisor Q-sort ratings of students' responsiveness to client feelings will be directly related to the degree to which personal feelings are expressed in reports of group supervision.

Prediction 6:   Responsiveness to the feelings of a client in a filmed counseling interview will be directly related to the degree to which personal feelings are expressed in reports of group supervision.

Research Method

Subjects.

The subjects were 26 students enrolled in the Introductory Practicum in Guidance at the Harvard Graduate School of Education, [5] February to May, 1965. The sample included six men and 20 women. Subjects ranged in age from twenty-one years to forty-eight years. All subjects had completed a theory course, an Introduction to Counseling, before entering the Practicum.

The Practicum included at least ten hours of counseling experience per week in a college, elementary, or secondary school setting. Subjects were supervised by personnel employed by the placement agencies and by experienced counselors employed by the university. Supervision was conducted both individually and in small groups of no more than six students each. The groups met weekly for approximately two hours.

Procedure

Corrected RIRS.

Students were given individually administered Rorschach tests during October, 1964. The protocols were then scored independently by Drs. George Spivack and Jules Spotts at the Devereux Foundation for Training and Research. The two resulting sets of ranks were compared by means of Spearman's rho. A correlation coefficient of $+.96$ was obtained.

Two subjects who appeared to the tester to be inordinately disturbed by the testing process and one who gave a large number of curious sexual responses were placed at the bottom of the RIRS.

Group Supervision Report Scale.

As part of the course work for the Introductory Practicum in Guidance, all subjects were required to submit a report of their own case presentation to their supervisory group which consisted, with but one exception, of six students and their supervisor. [6] These reports were rated for openness, the degree to which the reports contained references to the writers' personal feelings in regard to the counseling sessions presented or to the supervisory session itself.

The scale that was developed by the investigator (Appendix C) assigned the highest scores to reports in which the subject's own feelings were a central theme. Self-evaluation received less weight. Reports of evaluation of self by others merited an even lower rating. Those reports that dealt with matters wholly external to the reporter were assigned the lowest ratings.

5   All measures were not available for all subjects.

6   One supervisory group had only three members.

The reports submitted by the subjects were scored according to this scale by two independent raters. The two sets of scores were found to be correlated at the (rho) +.75 level. Although relatively low in terms of objective test standards, this level of interrater reliability is quite respectable for a projective test (Murstein, 1963; Zubin, Eron, and Schumer, 1965) and appears to be justified in view of the exploratory nature of the present research.

TABLE 9

BEHAVIORAL INDICATIONS OF PSYCHOLOGICAL CLOSEDNESS

(Subjects Reranked in Estimation of Psychological
Openness from the Rorschach Index of Repressive Style)

Subject	Ranking Given	Observations
ABC	Third from last.	Appeared to be very uneasy. Complained about the test. Tried to account for responses in terms of reading about the test. Most salient datum, high-pitched, strained laugh running throughout.
DEF	Next to last.	Good deal of belittling of the test. So belligerent was DEF in this situation that it appeared that she was being extremely threatened by it. In addition, she did a great deal of unusual gesticulating and vocalizing.
GHI	Last.	Gave 63 responses to the test. Eleven of these were sexual in character. The subject appeared to be somewhat agitated by her responses and attempted to justify them in terms of the fact that she had elementary school age children. Her distress was also inferred from her unusual posture. Through much of the test she appeared to be hiding from the examiner.

The resulting order was the Corrected Rorschach Index of Repressive Style. According to the rationale developed in that section above, it was considered that this behavior was *prima facie* evidence of a lack of *adaptive* openness.

Supervisors' Ratings.

At the end of the spring semester, each subject was rated by his Harvard supervisor on the seven-point scale (Appendix B) and on the Q-sort described above. Four of the five supervisors rated six students each; the fifth rated two students. All of the supervisors had received their training in counseling at the Harvard Graduate School of Education (HGSE) and were considered to be experienced counselors. Two had received the Ed. D. in Counseling Psychology at HGSE, one was the associate director of the Harvard Bureau of Study Counsel, and the remaining two supervisors were graduate students in the dissertation phase of their work at HGSE.

Subjects were rank ordered in terms of the ratings they received on the seven-point competence scale, and, again, in terms of the placement of Q-sort items dealing with the subject's general mode of responding to client feeling.

In the latter case, the placement of items 6, 12, 18, and 21 determined the score any given subject received. Item 6, as most indicative of a subject's responsiveness to client feeling, was given a weight of four. Item 12, indicating a somewhat lesser degree of responsiveness, was given a weight of three. Items 21 and 18 were weighted two and one respectively. Now, the higher the number of the column on the Q-sort in which an item is placed, the more typical of the subject the item is judged to be. Therefore, the weighted feeling score was derived from the supervisors' Q-sorts of subjects by multiplying the weights of items 6, 12, 18, and 21 by the numbers of the columns in which they were placed and summing the products. For example, let us say that A's supervisor placed item 6 in column 4, item 12 in column 6, item 21 in column 8, and item 18 in column 10. The computations in Table 10 would yield A's weighted score. Subjects were rank ordered in terms of their weighted Q-sort scores.

TABLE 10

COMPUTATION OF RESPONSIVENESS TO CLIENT FEELING SCORE
(Example)

Item	Item Weight		Column Placement		Item Score
6	4	x	4	=	16
12	3	x	6	=	18
21	2	x	8	=	16
18	1	x	10	=	10

A's Weighted Score	60

Responsiveness to Client Affect Scale.

In May, 1965, the sound film *A Clinical Picture of Claustrophobia* (Finesinger and Powdermaker, 1951) was presented to the subjects as a part of a regular class session of the course in Introductory Practicum in Guidance at the Harvard Graduate School of Education. Subjects were told that the film would be stopped 28 times during its showing and that, in each case, they were to write down the response they would make if they were dealing with the client in the film.

The resultant protocols were scored by two independent raters according to the method developed by the author (Appendix D). Subjects' responsiveness to feeling was determined by counting the number of responses which fit into any of the four "feeling categories," response to implicit feeling, reorganization of feeling, recognition of feeling, or questions concerning feeling.

Interrater reliability was assessed by means of correlating the two sets of ranks derived from a frequency count of the entries in the "feeling categories" made by each rater for each subject. The Spearman rho was $+.94$ ($N = 17$), which compares favorably with the reliabilities reported in similar studies, e.g., Kagan (1961); Seeman (1949); Snyder (1955); Strupp and Wallach (1965).

Summary

This chapter suggested possible operational definitions for the constructs which are the independent and dependent variables of the general hypothesis. Psychological openness was defined operationally in terms of the Corrected Rorschach Index of Repressive Style and the Group Supervision Report Scale. Effectiveness in counseling was defined operationally in terms of supervisory ratings and responsiveness to client affect in a simulated counseling situation.

Experimental predictions were formulated to test the strength of the general hypothesis that effectiveness in counseling is directly related to the psychological openness of the counselor. The methodology employed to test the predictions was described.

BIBLIOGRAPHY

Abeles, N. "A study of the characteristics of counselor trainees." Unpublished Doctoral Dissertation, University of Texas, 1958.

Allport, G. A. "The use of personal documents in psychological science," *Social Science Research Council Bulletin*, 1942, No. 49.

Berg, I. A., and H. E. Adams. "The experimental bases of personality assessment," in *Experimental Foundations of Clinical Psychology*, ed. A. J. Bachrach. New York: Basic Books, 1962, 52-96.

Bergman, D. "Counseling method and client responses," *Journal of Consulting Psychology, 15*, 1951, 216-224.

Bordin, E. S. *Psychological Counseling.* New York: Appleton-Century-Crofts, 1955.

Broudy, I., F. Greenwald, C. Johnson, S. Gann, C. Queller, K. Cogele, B. Wellstead, H. Greene, C. Avery, J. Knitzer, E. Rogoff, E. Newton, E. Goldman, M. Hogenson, L. Porter, and E. Williams. *The Congruence of Student and Faculty Conceptions of the Ideal Counselor.* Cambridge, Mass.: Unpublished paper, Harvard University, 1964.

Desrosches, H. F., and E. R. Larsen. "The Rorschach test as an index of the willingness and/or ability to communicate," *Journal of Clinical Psychology, 20*, 1964, 384-386.

Edwards, A. L. *The Social Desirability Variable in Personality Assessment and Research.* New York: Dryden, 1957.

Ellsworth, S. "The consistency of counselor feeling-verbalization," *Journal of Counseling Psychology, 10*, 1963, 356-361.

Eysenck, H. J. "La validite des techniques projectives," *Revue de Psychologie Applique, 5*, 1955, 231-234.

Fiedler, F. E. "A comparison of therapeutic relationships in psychoanalytic, nondirective, and Adlerian psychotherapy," *Journal of Consulting Psychology, 14*, 1950a, 433-445.

Fiedler, F. E. "The concept of an ideal therapeutic relationship," *Journal of Consulting Psychology, 14*, 1950b, 239-245.

Finesinger, J., and F. Powdermaker. *A Clinical Picture of Claustrophobia* (Motion Picture). Washington, D. C.: Veterans Administration, 1951.

Frank, G. H., and A. Sweetland. "A study of the process of psychotherapy," *Journal of Consulting Psychology, 26*, 1962, 135-138.

Frank, G. H. "The role of cognitions in illness and healing," in *Research in Psychotherapy*, eds. H. H. Strupp and L. Luborsky, V.II. Washington, D. C.: American Psychological Association, 1962.

Gardner, R., P. S. Holzman, G. A. Klein, H. Linton, and D. P. Spence. "Cognitive control: A study of individual consistencies in cognitive behavior," *Psychological Issues, 1*, 1959, No. 4.

Hartshorne, H., and M. A. May. *Studies in Deceit.* New York: Macmillian, 1928.

Holt, R. R. *Manual for the Scoring of Primary Process Manifestations in Rorschach Responses.* Draft 8. New York University: Research Center for Mental Health, 1960 (mimeo).

Holt, R. R., and Goldberger, L. "Personological correlates of reactions to perceptual isolation," *WADC Technical Report*, 1959, 59-739.

Holt, R. R., and L. L. Luborsky, *Personality Patterns of Psychiatrists: A Study of Methods for Selecting Residents.* V. I. New York: Basic Books, 1958.

Holzman, P. S., and R. W. Gardner. "Leveling and repression," *Journal of Abnormal and Social Psychology, 59*, 1959, 151-155.

Kagan, J. "Stylistic variables in fantasy behavior: The ascription of affect states to social stimuli," in *Contemporary Issues in Thematic Apperception Methods*, eds. J. Kagan and G. Lesser, Springfield, Illinois: Charles C. Thomas, 1961, 196-220.

Kagan, J., and G. Lesser. (eds.). *Contemporary Issues in Thematic Apperceptive Methods*. Springfield, Illinois: Charles C. Thomas, 1961.

Kelly, E. L., and D. W. Fiske. *The Prediction of Performance in Clinical Psychology*. Ann Arbor, Michigan: University of Michigan Press, 1951.

Kerlinger, F. N. *Foundations of Behavior Research*. New York: Holt, Rinehart and Winston, 1964.

Kirtner, W. L., and D. S. Cartwright. "Success and failure in client-centered therapy as a function of initial in-therapy behavior," *Journal of Consulting Psychology, 22*, 1959, 329-333.

Levine, M., and G. Spivack. *The Rorschach Index of Repressive Style*. Springfield, Ill.: Charles C. Thomas, 1964.

Marlowe, D., and D. Crowne. *Approval Motive: Studies in Evaluation Dependency*. New York: Wiley, 1964.

Masling, J. "The influence of situational and interpersonal variables in projective testing," *Psychological Bulletin, 57*, 1960, 65-85.

Murstein, B. I. *Theory and Research in Projective Techniques (Emphasizing the TAT)*. New York: Wiley, 1963.

Porter, E. H. *Introduction to Therapeutic Counseling*. Boston: Houghton Mifflin, 1950.

Rogers, C. R. *Counseling and Psychotherapy*. Boston: Houghton Mifflin, 1942.

Rogers, C. R. "The development of insight in a counseling relationship," *Journal of Consulting Psychology, 8*, 1944, 331-341.

Rogers, C. R. *On Becoming a Person*. Boston: Houghton Mifflin, 1961.

Rottschafer, R. H., and G. A. Renjalia. "Relationship of dependent-like verbal behaviors to counseling style and induced set," *Journal of Consulting Psychology, 26*, 1962, 172-177.

Schafer, R. *Psychoanalytic Interpretation in Rorschach Testing*. New York: Grune and Stratton, 1954.

Seeman, J. A. "A study of the process of nondirective therapy," *Journal of Consulting Psychology, 13*, 1949, 157-168.

Schaffer, L. F. "Review of the Rorschach test," in *The Fifth Mental Measurements Yearbook*, ed. O. K. Buros, Highland Park, New Jersey: Gryphon, 1959.

Silverman, L. H. "Regression in the service of the ego: A case study," *Journal of Projective Techniques, 29*, 1965, 232-242.

Snyder, W. U. *Casebook of Non-Directive Counseling*. Boston: Houghton Mifflin Co., 1947.

Snyder, W. U. "An investigation of the nature of non-directive psychotherapy," *Journal of Genetic Psychology, 33*, 1945, 193-223.

Snyder, W. U. "The personality of clinical students," *Journal of Counseling Psychology, 2,* 1955, 47-52.

Speisman, J. C. "Depth of interpretation and verbal resistance in psychotherapy," *Journal of Consulting Psychology, 23,* 1959, 93-99.

Stephenson, W. *The Study of Behavior: Q-Technique and Its Methodology.* Chicago: University of Chicago Press, 1953.

Strupp, H. H., and M. S. Wallach. "A further study of psychiatrists' responses in quasi-therapy situations," *Behavioral Science, 10,* 1965, 113-134.

Sundberg, N. D. "The practice of psychological testing in clinical services in the United States," *American Psychologist, 16,* 1961, 79-83.

Super, D. S. "Theories and assumptions underlying approaches to personality assessment," in *Objective Approaches to Personality Assessment,* eds. B. M. Bass and I. A. Berg, Princeton, New Jersey: Van Nostrand, 1959, 24-41.

Tutko, T. A. "The need for social approval and its effect on responses to projective tests." Unpublished Doctoral Dissertation, Ohio State University, 1962.

Witkin, H. A., H. B. Lewis, M. Hertzman, K. Machover, P. B. Neissner, and S. Wapner. *Personality Through Perception.* New York: Harper, 1954.

Wolberg, L. R. *The Techniques of Psychotherapy.* New York: Grune and Stratton, 1954.

Zubin, J., L. D. Eron, and F. Schumer. *An Experimental Approach to Projective Techniques.* New York: Wiley, 1965.

7

Psychological Openness and Counselor Effectiveness: Results of Pilot Study

Inspection of Table 11 reveals that the Prediction One, that supervisor ratings of the overall competence characteristic of student counselors would be directly related to Corrected RIRS, received clear support. On the other hand, Prediction Two, that supervisor ratings of the responsiveness of student counselors to the feelings of clients would be related to the Corrected RIRS, failed to receive support. However, the results, in regard to Prediction Three, which posit a direct relationship between the Corrected RIRS and responses to the feeling of a client in a filmed interview, are equivocal and require further examination.

Table 11 further reveals the Group Supervision Report Scale (GSRS) positively relates with supervisor ratings of both overall competence and responsiveness to client view.

This chapter will describe the results of the predictions testing the relationship between counseling effectiveness and psychological openness. The results will be presented according to the measuring instrument employed to assess psychological openness.

The Corrected Rorschach Index of Repressive Style

Prediction One: Supervisor ratings of student counselors for overall competence will be directly related to the Corrected Rorschach Index of Repressive Style. *Result:* Both supervisor ratings and Corrected RIRS scores were available for 17 students. A rank order correlation (rho) of +.455 was obtained. A correlation of this magnitude is statistically significant beyond the .05 level.

Prediction Two: Supervisor ratings of the responsiveness of student counselors to the feelings of clients will be directly related to the Corrected RIRS. Both of these scores were obtainable for seventeen subjects. *Result:* A rank order correlation (rho) of +.312. The probability of obtaining a coefficient of this magnitude from two unrelated variables is greater than .10.

Prediction Three: The responsiveness of students to the feelings of a client in a filmed counseling interview will be directly related to the Corrected RIRS. *Result:* Both sets of scores were available for 17 subjects. A rank order (rho) correlation of +.339 was obtained. The probability of obtaining a correlation of this magnitude from two unrelated variables is less than .10 but greater than .05.

Thus, one of the predictions (Prediction One) was clearly sustained and another (Prediction Two) was clearly not sustained. However, the results in regard to Prediction Three are more equivocal. While they fail to reach the conventional .05 level of statistical significance, they are nonetheless to be expected on the basis of chance less than ten times out of 100. Consequently, this prediction would seem both to require and deserve further examination.

TABLE 11

The Relationship of Effectiveness in Counseling
to Psychological Openness
(Spearman Rho Rank Order Correlation Coefficient)

Effectiveness in Counseling	Psychological Openness					
	Corrected RIRS			Group Supervision Report Scale		
Supervisors' Ratings for Overall Competence	N	Rho	P[a]	N	Rho	P[a]
	17	+.455	.05	24	+.531	.01
Supervisors' Ratings for Response to Client Feeling	17	+.312	.10	24	+.428	.025
Response to Client Affect Scale (Film)	17	+.399	.10 .05	19	+.199	.10

[a] One-tailed tests.

Group Supervision Report Scale

Three predictions were made utilizing the Group Supervision Report Scale as an index of psychological openness.

Prediction Four: Supervisor ratings of student counselors for overall competence will be directly related to the degree to which personal feelings are expressed in group reports. *Result:* Supervisor ratings and Group Supervision Report Scale scores were available for 24 subjects. A correlation coefficient (rho) of +.531 was obtained. The expectation for obtaining a coefficient this large by chance is less than one in 100.

Prediction Five: Supervisor ratings of the responsiveness of student counselors to client feelings is directly related to the degree to which personal feelings are expressed in Group Reports. *Result:* Weighted Q-sort scores and Group Supervision Report Scale scores were available for 24 subjects. A rank order (rho) correlation of +.428 was obtained. The probability of obtaining a coefficient of this size by chance alone is less than .025.

Prediction Six: The responsiveness of student feelings to a client in a filmed counseling interview will be directly related to the degree to which personal feelings are expressed in reports of group supervision. *Result:* Film response scores and Group Supervision Report Scale scores were available for 19 subjects. A rank order (rho) correlation of +.199 was obtained. A coefficient this large might be expected to occur more than 20 times in 100 by chance alone.

Discussion

According to the results presented above, Supervisors' Competence Ratings were significantly related to the Corrected RIRS in this sample. In other words, there was a definite tendency for counseling students who gave more elaborate and specific responses to the Rorschach technique and who did not exhibit any unusual behavior in conjunction with the test, to receive higher ratings for overall competence from their practicum supervisors.

The question arises concerning the extent to which this relationship is attributable to the identification of psychological openness and the extent to which it is attributable to the identification of psychological closedness. This question can be answered, in part, by means of reference to the correlation obtained between the RIRS uncorrected for behavioral indications of psychological closedness and supervisor judgments. The uncorrected RIRS is correlated (rho) +.135 with supervisor judgments of overall competence. Thus, it seems that the predictive power of the Corrected RIRS in regard to ratings of overall competence hangs heavily upon the identification of psychologically closed subjects.

These results might be understood in terms of the findings by Stern, Stein, and Bloom (1956) in regard to the "synthetic" approach to personality assessment. It appears that assessment which proceeds from a hypothetical psychological model tends to be most effective in identifying sub-groups of persons who lie near the extremes of the distribution, persons for whom the model is particularly relevant —in either a positive or a negative sense. There is, as the authors point out, no guarantee that a substantial number of persons at both ends of the continuum will be found in any given sample. Thus one might conclude that the psychologically open pole of the continuum is irrelevant for this particular sample, that the single important datum provided by the corrected RIRS is psychological closedness, which might be utilized as a "cutoff score."

However, it is fully conceivable that these results are, in fact, more a function of the characteristics of the criterion than of the predictor. That is, there is a distinct possibility that the supervisors were able to identify students who were clearly incompetent with considerably more success than they could discriminate among more effective students. It is certainly true that the most easily interpreted feedback from the staffs of the agencies where students are placed is negative in character. In regard to students of moderate ability the feedback tends to be ambiguous in nature. While the very poor student often gives himself away quite readily, it is frequently difficult to obtain the information necessary to make the more subtle distinctions among the performances of able persons.

The results reveal no clear-cut relationship between the Corrected RIRS and supervisor Q-sorts of counselors' Responsiveness to Client Affect. However, the Corrected RIRS comes much closer to the mark (rho = +.312) than the uncorrected RIRS (rho = +.070). Again it appears that the success of this method depends, in the main, upon the identification of psychologically closed students.

Although the coefficient of correlation between the Corrected RIRS and the responsiveness of subjects to a client in a quasi-counseling situation (RCAS) failed to reach the conventional .05 level of significance by a narrow margin, the relationship revealed appears to be worthy of notice. The two correlated (rho) +.399 (p < .10). Given the difficulty of the present prediction problem, that of anticipating the performance of students in a complex task by means of a single approximation made seven months in advance of the criterion measure, the relationship seems to take on added importance.[1]

What is more, an analysis of the results in terms of "hits and misses" reveals that the Corrected RIRS successfully classified subjects in terms of RCAS scores at a level beyond the .05 level of significance. That is, six of the eight subjects having Corrected RIRS score falling above the median had RCAS scores exceeding the median of that distribution. Likewise, six of the eight subjects falling below the Corrected RIRS median fell below the RCAS median. Hence, 12 of the 16 subjects[2] were "hits" and four were "misses." Since the probability of placing any one of the subjects into the correct RCAS group was .5, the binomial test (P = Q = 1/2) was employed. The probability of 12 correct placements in 16 attempts occurring by chance is .038 (one-tailed test).

Hence, it appears that it is possible to discriminate between high and low RCAS groups beyond the conventional level of significance. It should further be noted that the uncorrected RIRS discriminates these groups at the same level of significance. This suggests that the prediction of responsiveness to client affect does not depend solely on the identification of psychologically closed subjects so much as on

---

[1] It might be argued that the restricted nature of the study sample, the subjects were survivors of the HGSE screening process, militated against a larger correlation by reducing the range of ability (Cronbach, 1960, p. 352f). Since the formulae for the correction of correlations from restricted samples assume a normal distribution, a Pearson r, and require information concerning the variance of scores from the larger population—in this case, including those applicants for the counseling program at Harvard who were rejected—they are not applicable to the present research (Guilford, 1956, p. 332).

[2] The seventeenth subject fell at the median of the Corrected RIRS distribution and was therefore deleted from the analysis (Siegal, 1956, p. 112).

the identification of the several degrees of psychological openness. It lends credence to the notion that the psychologically open segment of the psychologically open-psychologically closed continuum is relevant to this sample. Conversely, doubt is cast upon the attempt to explain the dependence of the correlation of the Corrected RIRS with supervisors' ratings upon the identification of closed subjects in terms of the irrelevancy of high RIRS scores to the present sample. As a result, added weight must be given to the alternative notion that the supervisors' judgments may be at fault in this case.

Additional Predictors

In contrast to the successful predictions of effectiveness emanating from the theory of psychological openness, none of the standard predictors currently employed by the Harvard Graduate School of Education were found to be significantly related to the criteria (Table 12). Neither collegiate grade point average, nor Harvard Percentile on the Miller Analogies Test nor the Graduate Record Examination, nor number of psychology courses taken correlated with any of the criteria at a level exceeding chance expectancy. As a result, the ranking of students by the Admissions Committee (which correlated +.662 and +.645 with college GPA and Harvard MAT/GRE percentile) bore no significant relationship to any of the criteria.

TABLE 12

ACADEMIC PREDICTORS OF COUNSELOR EFFECTIVENESS

(Spearman Rho Correlation Coefficients)

Predictors	Counselor Effectiveness								
	Supervisors' Competence Ratings			Responsiveness to Client Feeling Scale (Q-sort)			Responsiveness to Client Affect Scale (Film)		
	N	Rho	p[a]	N	Rho	p[a]	N	Rho	p[a]
Undergraduate (Jr./Sr.) Grade Point Average	17	−.036	.25	15	+.002	.50	15	+.129	.25
Number of Psychology Courses Taken	20	+.221	.125	20	+.008	.50	20	+.005	.50
Percentile GRE/MAT	18	+.270	.125	18	+.148	.25	16	+.172	.25
Admissions Committee Ratings	19	+.143	.25	19	+.108	.25	17	−.116	.25

[a]One-tailed test.

It might be argued in favor of current procedures that the correlations were taken from a restricted sample. That is, since the subjects dealt with in this study have already been screened on academic grounds, it might be objected that the true value of the academic predictors has been masked (Guilford, 1956). However, this argument is blunted somewhat by the fact that, despite preselection, there remains appreciable variation in the predictor variables (Table 13) and in the criterion variables. Of course, a test of the predictors on all applicants rather than a selected sample is most desirable. Nevertheless, it is clear that in regard to the present sample, the measures for psychological openness control a significant amount of the variance of the criterion measures of counseling effectiveness; the measures of academic aptitude and the ratings of the Admissions Committee based on them do not.

TABLE 13

The Parameters of Academic Predictors of Success in Guidance Used By the Harvard Graduate School of Education Admission Committee
(Descriptive Statistics)

Variable	N	Range	Mean	Median	Standard Deviation
HGSE percentile, GRE-V/ Mat	18	4-91	65.8333	69.5	18.7374
Weighted GPS, Jr. and Sr. years	17	1.7-3.8	2.9	3.000	.0596
Number of Psych. courses	20	1-30	6.35	4.000	6.95

Consequently, it would appear that the present study provides some empirical support for the asseveration that the personality style of the counselor is a crucial variable in counseling. Proceeding from a theoretical conception of the nature of the personality organization prerequisite to the capacity to respond effectively to clients' affective communications, it was possible to predict the value of several important measures of counselor effectiveness with some accuracy. This suggests that this conception of the personality of the counselor is a potentially useful one for further research concerned with the counseling process.

TABLE 14

Intercorrelations of Academic Predictors of Success in Counseling
And Admissions Committee Ratings of Subjects
(Spearman Rho Correlation Coefficients)

	HGSE percentile, Graduate Record Exam/Miller Analogies Test			Weighted GPA, Jr. and Sr.			Number of Psychology Courses Taken		
	N	Rho	p^a	N	Rho	p^a	N	Rho	p^a
Admissions Committee Ratings	16	+.645	.005	17	+.662	.005	18	+.319	.05
HGSE Percentile GRE/MAT				16	+.712	.005	17	+.319	.10
Weighted GPA, Jr. and Sr.							16	+.483	.05
Number of Psychology Courses									

Summary

In this chapter, the results of the present investigation were presented and discussed. The results provided evidence in support of four of the six predictions drawn from the general hypothesis. First, the supervisors' ratings of overall competence in counseling were found to be significantly related to the Corrected RIRS. Second, the Corrected RIRS was successful in distinguishing between subjects who responded more frequently to the feelings of a client in a motion picture (high RCAS) and those who responded less frequently in this manner (low RCAS). Third, GSRS scores correlated significantly with supervisors' ratings of overall competence and of responsiveness to client feeling. On the other hand, no significant relationships were found to obtain between the Corrected RIRS and supervisors' ratings for responsiveness to client-feeling nor between the GSRS and the RCAS.

Several of the academic variables used in the selection of students were compared with the measures of counselor effectiveness. No significant findings were produced. Admission committee ratings were not found to be significantly related to counselor effectiveness. The effect of the preselection of subjects for admission to HGSE upon the statistical technique (rank order correlation) used was discussed.

BIBLIOGRAPHY

Cronbach, L. J. *Essentials of Psychological Testing.* 2nd ed. New York: Harper and Row, 1960.

Guilford, J. P. *Fundamental Statistics in Psychology and Education.* New York: McGraw-Hill, 1956.

Siegel, S. *Nonparametric Statistics.* New York: McGraw-Hill, 1956.

Stern, G., M. Stein, and B. Bloom. *Methods in Personality Assessment.* Glencoe, Illinois: Free Press, 1956.

SECTION IV

SUMMARY:
SELECTION OF COUNSELORS

8

Summary:
Selection of Counselors

The foregoing chapters have presented two somewhat related but distinct theories in regard to the contribution of the counselor's personality to the counseling process. Both theories were put to empirical test and, in both cases, the results were in accord with the predictions drawn from the respective theories. So what?

It is certainly obvious that neither theory has yet achieved a high level of confirmation. The sample was small and more extensive replications by other investigators in other settings remain to be done.

A more serious problem, from the standpoint of counselor selection, however, is that posed by the criteria employed. They are, in each case, "proximate"; the relationship between them and client benefit is merely putative. Counselor trainees were deemed "effective" when they behaved in a way consistent with the beliefs of their supervisors. The nature of these beliefs should be clear from the rating instruments themselves. Although they are obviously ones that have a wide currency in professional circles, there is virtually no systematic evidence to confirm their validity clearly.

We believe that the clients of counselors who are more highly regarded by their supervisors and are more responsive to client feeling will derive more benefit from counseling than those who are treated by counselors obtaining lower ratings on these dimensions. To date, the record of attempts to demonstrate the validity of this general belief-system has not been impressive, e.g., Eysenck, 1960; Volsky, Magoon, Norman, and Hoyt, 1965. But, at the same time, it is not totally devoid of success. Consider, for example, the findings of Vosbeck (1959), of Dickenson and Truax (1966), and of Gilbreath (1967). In each case, there is evidence that counseling conducted along lines parallel to our assumptions benefited clients sufficiently to be of consequence to their academic performance in college.

Nevertheless, encouraging findings are rare in the literature. For instance, Gilbreath (1967) cites 13 studies concerned with the group counseling of underachievers, only three of which reported positive findings. When one considers how much more likely "successful studies" are to find their way into print, the urgent need for replicating the forementioned experiments prior to taking their findings too seriously becomes clear.

Moreover, our studies can derive comfort from this research only "by association," as it were. That is, they are apparently based on similar principles to those represented in the rating scales, but one cannot be certain that it was the principles which were efficacious, or simply the nature of the persons who acted as the therapists in the studies, or an interaction of the two factors. The answer to this question has, of course, important implications for the generalizability of the results.

What is plainly required are studies which relate the "proximate" criteria, supervisor judgments and performance on various analogous tasks commonly applied in counselor education programs, to the ultimate criterion, the actual benefit which clients derive from the counselor. There are likely to be, if existing findings are reliable guideposts, appreciable individual differences among faculty supervisors in this regard (Allen, 1964). Further, these differences may well be unrelated to the other skills which make a person a desirable supervisor: depth of theoretical understanding, personal warmth, and therapeutic acumen.[1] Obviously, there is a need for the calibration of supervisors in regard to the assessment of outcome and for the investigation of the utility of the other criteria of "effectiveness."

Patterson (1967) asserts that an adequately validated set of "proximate criteria" are presently at hand. The reference is to the work done in regard to the "therapeutic triad" posited by Rogers (1957; 1961). Patterson suggests that research on these variables (accurate empathy—AE; therapist genuineness or congruence—GEN; unconditional positive regard/nonpossessive warmth—NPW) has reached the stage where they can be employed with confidence, as evidence of counselor effectiveness. If a counselor trainee attains a high level of performance on the scales measuring AE, GEN, and NPW, one can confidently assert that his personal counseling will be of appreciable benefit to his clients. These scales then would appear to provide the Archimedean point upon which selection procedures may be founded. As Patterson (1968) puts it,

> We are thus in a position where a usable criterion exists, which makes possible predictive studies. It is now necessary to find, or develop, predictive measures.

---

[1] The skill involved in assessing the effect which a counselor has had on a client is largely that of being able to predict the behavior of the client subsequent to counseling. This skill has been the subject of much inquiry under the heading of "interpersonal perception." It would seem that one of the most plausible conclusions that may be drawn from this imposing mass of literature is that some persons are, indeed, able to predict the behavior of others with considerable accuracy, but that the ability to do so is largely independent of training in counseling or therapy (Luft, 1950; Taft, 1950; 1955), clinical experience (Kelly and Fiske, 1951; Soskin, 1954), and proficiency in helping clients (Lesser, 1961). However, it is frequently assumed that these skills are facets of a single factor. Consequently, it is supposed that the supervisor is a reasonable judge of how useful the counselor trainee was to the practicum clients with whom he worked. But such a judgment entails an inference in regard to the clients' extra-counseling behavior for which his expertise in anticipating within counseling behavior seems to be of little value or even, as Sarbin, Taft, and Bailey (1960) suggest, a definite hindrance.

Certainly, one can only agree that the Rogers, Truax, Carkhuff *et al.* research concerning the therapeutic worth of the conditions measured by the AE, GEN, and NPW scales represents a pioneering step. Further, the use of ratings taken from these scales as criteria for the determination of students' "effectiveness in counseling" has more to recommend it than the bulk of present procedures.

Nevertheless, there are problems here which suggest that Patterson's ebullience is somewhat premature. Take, for instance, his statement that AE, GEN, and NPW "have demonstrated to be sufficient conditions for therapeutic personality change" (1967, p. 506). Translated back into the terms of the data from which it was abstracted, this statement would read something like the following: "ratings of counselor behavior in terms of the AE, the GEN, and the NPW have consistently accounted for some 10 to 25 per cent of the variance of certain phases of Q-sort, MMPI, and Rorschach behavior of the clients involved and of the scores on measures of the amount of introspection in which they indulge."

Obviously this definition of "therapeutic personality change" is not exceedingly compelling. Much room for dissent is left due to the conspicuous shortcomings of the instruments employed. Furthermore, only a small part of the total variance is accounted for and it is not at all clear, excepting the Dickenson and Truax study (1966), that practically significant changes were wrought as a function of these variables. [2]

Consequently, while this research represents a laudable beginning to a difficult and important undertaking, only the most tentative conclusions can be drawn. That is, a number of important issues have been raised, but unequivocal answers are still lacking. At most, the present research offers some support for the nearly universal belief that the quality of the interpersonal relationship between the client and the counselor can have effects on the outcome of treatment.

It is apparent, then, that it would be a serious error to suppose that we have an adequate solution to the criterion problem at hand. There is, however, a real danger of such a supposition being made. It is, for instance, much more convenient to employ a criterion which depends solely upon verbal behavior from counseling sessions themselves than to trace the behavioral consequences of counseling that occur *in vivo*. But until an appreciably greater overlap of Rogers' "Therapeutic triad" with specific behavioral objectives of the type which bring people into counseling can be demonstrated, Patterson's suggestion cannot be taken seriously.

---

[2] For instance, consider the study by Truax (1966) to which Patterson refers. The criteria consisted of various Q-sorts and special scales derived from the MMPI. The three therapeutic conditions were found to be significantly related to these indicators of adjustment. The correlations ranged from .48-.31. To say that this study provides a piece of solid evidence in support of the proposition that the independent variables are "sufficient conditions" for "therapeutic personality change" is to be overexpansive. Although there are studies here and there which link Q-sort and MMPI performance to behavioral criteria, the magnitude of these relationships is similar to that between the therapeutic triad and the tests. As a result, caution is clearly indicated. Since both the therapeutic conditions and the behavioral referents of any meaningful definition of therapeutic personality change have such meager overlaps with the tests, it is clearly possible that they share little or no common variance.

Indeed, there is a rapidly growing body of evidence which suggests that at least insofar as one is concerned with overt behavior—which includes most of the objectives to which guidance refers when soliciting public support—the "interview model" is an inappropriate one. The data at hand indicate that a "consultation model" provides much more ready access to these goals. [3]

Much of the work of the so-called "behavior modifiers" may be subsumed under this rubric. Their concern is not with the origins of any given educational/behavioral problem. Instead they attempt to discern what it is *in the contemporaneous school situation* that maintains the undesirable behavior. On the basis of such an analysis, they help the teacher (and perhaps, parents and other school personnel) develop and implement a plan of action. Given the operant assumptions of the "behavior modifiers," the analysis is likely to have taken into account the typical *consequences* of the target behavior. Accordingly the remedial strategy or program will probably be structured to alter these consequences and, further, to modify the consequences of the competing behaviors which are more desirable in character. Take, for example, the following case (Baer, 1967).

A child was noticeably uncooperative with her preschool classmates. Her interaction with other children was generally brief and hostile. She spent 50 per cent of her time within three feet of other children, but only two per cent of it in cooperation with them. Twenty per cent of her time was taken up with teacher. Remediation seemed in order. No attempt was made to engage the child in traditional psychotherapy, to get her into the "pressurized cabin" (Redl, 1966) where the intrapsychic sources of her difficulties might be determined and changed. However, her teachers were encouraged to shower her with "unconditional positive regard." Although they evidently undertook this task with some enthusiasm, cooperative behavior had increased to 40 per cent. In order to test the assumption that it was indeed the contingency which was crucial, the teachers returned to a noncontingent schedule of social reinforcement. Cooperative behavior rapidly dropped to five per cent. Thereafter, the teachers employed the contingency approach until the natural rewards of cooperation took firm control.

Baer's example is illustrative of the "behavior modification" approach. The emphasis is unequivocally upon the alteration of some aspect of the environment in which the unwanted behavior occurs so as to change the "meaning" which it has to the subject. The "behavior modifier" provides a program for doing this, and those persons naturally in that situation generally carry it out. That is, they alter some facet of their normal response to the child in the course of their regular work with him as a parent, teacher, or principal. Amendments in the program are made in light of fluctuations in the rate at which the target behavior is emitted, not in terms of speculations derived from the transactions of a therapy hour. Krasner

---

3 By "consultation model" we mean those approaches to educational problems whose main efforts are directed toward a "reprogramming" of the child's educational environment rather than toward a rearrangement of psychic forces within him by such means as personal counseling.

and Ullman (1965), Ullman and Krasner (1965), and Whelan (1966) provide further illustrations of this line of thought.

Recently, another "consultative approach" to the problems of the public school emerged. Sarason *et al.* (1966) describe their venture into the public schools of New Haven. Their very promising work also represents a break with the traditional "pressurized cabin" model of rendering assistance. They tenaciously resisted attempts of school personnel to cast them in the traditional roles—as test-report generators or as take-him-out-of-the-room-and-adjust-internal-forces workers. Rather, they sought to understand what it was within the school that promoted the troublesome situation and, moreover, how the natural resources of the school could be invoked to remedy it. Their findings support the notion that at this juncture the "consultation model" has more to recommend it than the more orthodox mental health procedures.

The point is that it is more than just possible that the person who is well suited for the vis-à-vis mode of treatment is not necessarily favorably equipped to function as a consultant. Consequently, the separation of selection procedures from the ultimate indicators of success, observable change in clients, by means of increased emphasis on such proximate criteria as we have employed and those which Patterson suggests must be overcome. Research is urgently required which will relate various personality variables directly to change in the client behavior which justified the initiation of counseling.

Since the "behavioral-consultative format" appears to be the treatment of choice for effecting the changes in behavior most often sought by educational institutions, can we now dispense with the sort of thinking and research presented in the foregoing chapters? At this point in the development of our knowledge, it seems that one would be obliged to answer in the affirmative only if he were to agree that relatively limited, discrete bits of overt behavior alone are justifiable goals for counseling. It is, of course, true that the modification of certain rather sharply delimited behaviors can have far-reaching ramifications in a person's life. For instance, successful sphincter training may have extensive effects on the personality of an enuretic child. It allows for the disappearance of the anxiety, the shame, and self-deprecation which the incontinence occasions. Similarly, a stutterer may change considerably as he becomes more fluent. He may, for example, become much more social and, as a result, less depressed. Also, it must be confessed that the appeal to vague, highly inferential, intrapsychic variables has been badly abused by traditional approaches to counseling.

Nevertheless, it is far from evident that an affirmative response to the foregoing query (should we abandon the type of thinking from which cognitive flexibility and psychological openness emerge?) is required. For changes in specific overt behaviors are obviously not the only legitimate goals for counseling, as the behaviorists often suggest. They seem, frequently, to fall prey to the all-too-human proclivity of converting a useful technology into a metaphysic. Or, to put it another way, the behaviorists are wont to give ontological significance to what is basically a methodological tour de force. The tendency is to say that since some important things can be accomplished without reference to human subjectivity, the reality of subjective factors is so problematic as to make them unsuitable as outcome criteria. But such a view, while appealing in some ways, is hardly tenable. First, Joseph Wood Krutch (1965) has observed that skepticism is more reasonable in regard to events in the external and environment than in regard to one's own subjectivity (*vide:* Descartes' *Cogito ergo sum*). There is nothing else that we know as directly as our own subjectivity. Second, there is a definite suspicion that the behavior modifiers do themselves depend heavily upon extrapolations from their own subjective experience to that of others in the formulation of specific modification programs. The analysis of the various situations, the choice of reinforcers, and the determination of contingencies all frequently bear the stamp of such an extrapolation. Finally, attempts to deal with human behavior in operant terms have almost inevitably been forced to make concessions to subjective factors. Farber (1963) and Bijou and Baer (1961), for instance, recognize that the reinforcing potentialities of a given stimulus depend to a large degree on the *meaning* which it has for the particular subject involved. In sum, it would seem that we have more reason to believe that processes similar to those which we experience directly as individual human beings exist and are present in others than we do to accept the most reputable assertions of physical science, let alone those of the behaviorists!

The conclusion, then, is that there are legitimate objectives beyond those dealt with most effectively by behavioral techniques. Indeed, such things as the following clearly seem to be worthy objectives. There is, for example, the clarification of a person's internal frame of reference, the exposition of his basic assumptions about existence, his philosophy of life. There is the development of means to deal with the anxiety generated by guilt, meaninglessness, and the threat of death (Tillich, 1952). There is the unraveling of the various conflicting forces that make the development of a viable sense of identity difficult (Erikson, 1959).

Obviously, the model of treatment to which the criteria in the foregoing studies have reference is more germane to these issues. Hence, there appear to be solid grounds for rejecting any simple, monistic solution to the criterion problem in guidance, counseling, and psychotherapy, as tempting as the behaviorist a solution may be. What is more, the variety of defensible goals for counseling justifies the maintenance of a number of different sets of strategies. The nonbehavioral objectives bespeak a verbal-insight approach. On the other hand, the need to modify overt behavior is presently best satisfied by the various forms of behavior therapy.

This poses a new problem for selection and training. One general plan of selecting and educating students who will function in widely varied professional roles is plainly inappropriate, the fact that they may all be referred to as "counselors" or "psychotherapists" notwithstanding. There are, for instance, professional roles for which the main expectation is behavior modification. In such cases, elaborate training in the use of orthodox measures for dealing with clients in a standard interview situation is suspect. The question then might also be raised in regard to the relevance of such variables as openness and flexibility.

At present there are no satisfactory answers to this question, only speculation. It may well be that they are characteristics which contribute to success in the development and implementation of modification programs. This position has theoretical support, but it is after all an empirical question which has yet to be resolved experimentally. There is more reason, however, to believe that these variables are related to competence in helping clients achieve goals which cannot be so parsimoniously dealt with in the behaviorist's system.

Of perhaps greater interest is the fact that, while the case of recognizing no single set of desiderata for counseling as exhaustive is strong, training at any given institution almost invariably fixates on a single methodology. It is generally some form of the verbal-evocative model, and not infrequently the client-centered model, that prevails. The difficulty with such a state of affairs is that the roles for which students are being certified frequently exceed the limits of any particular methodology.This is to say that the tasks which are set for the various forms of the counseling profession are rarely, if ever, identical with those of any individual theory.

Consider the school counselor who has been carefully trained in client-centered counseling. He has been prepared to help persons explore and accept their inner worlds. This is patently, in our view, a most useful function. However, the expectations of the school for him are likely to go far beyond this function. Not all that is demanded of him has validity, of course. For example, roles of informer or enforcer for the administration are difficult to fit into a profession which values individual freedom and creative diversity more than institutional sovereignty, stereotypy, and conformity. But there are others which seem more reasonable such as, promoting socialization in an extremely belligerent child or in a withdrawn one and extending the amount of time spent attending to academic work. However, these are much less likely to yield to discussions of affective states than to carefully constructed behavior modification programs.

In such instances, the counselor's role demands that he utilize methods of the latter type, but his training has more than likely given him but a single tool. Worse, it may well have biased him against the consideration of any others. Consequently, we are confronted with the spectacle of a workman attempting to drive nails with a screwdriver and another struggling to loosen a bolt with a hammer. In each case, the particular tool was that favored, if not apotheosized, by his training institution.

It appears obvious, then, that the demands of the counselor's role cannot be contained within the boundaries of any single theory or school of thought. There is, however, the apparent assumption that either one must demonstrate that this theory and/or method can do virtually everything that is worth doing or that it be cast aside as superficial. Such thinking has led to spectacles like those created by the foregoing workmen.

Several alternatives are available. One is that counselors restrict themselves to cases where there is relatively unequivocal agreement between the goals to which their particular approach to counseling is most closely related and those to which the client aspires. Another would involve intensive training in a wide range of methodologies. This alternative may, of course, suffer from the difficulty mentioned above, that aptitudes for the various relevant methods may be unrelated or even, perhaps, inversely correlated. Nonetheless, such a solution to the problem appears to be the most practical in regard to the public schools. It would probably extend the period of time required for training, but the extension could be minimized by increasing the intensiveness of the curriculum—something for which the social sciences (and education and psychology in particular) have not been noted.

Either of these alternatives would, of course, be greatly enhanced by the systematic acquisition of empirically derived information concerning the merits of each of the various methodologies in regard to operationally defined goals for carefully specified populations. The matter of such an enterprise has been discussed elsewhere and is now under close scrutiny by the authors.

In sum, the foregoing studies point, we believe, to promising modes of anticipating the performance of counselors in regard to certain limited but important client goals.[4] More plainly, it appears that insofar as the objectives of counseling are changes in the subjective state of client, e.g., the reduction of guilt or shame, or even more directly, the development of a viable sense of identity, cognitive flexibility and psychological openness are promising variables to consider in the selection of students for training in counseling.

BIBLIOGRAPHY

Allen, T. W. "Empathy as a crucial variable in the counseling relationship." Unpublished qualifying paper, Harvard University, 1964.

Baer, D. "Behavior modification in pre-school settings." Paper given at the Ninth Annual Institute for Research in Clinical Psychology, University of Kansas, April, 1967.

Bijou, S. W., and D. M. Baer. *Child Development I: A Systematic and Empirical Theory.* New York: Appleton-Century-Crofts, 1961.

Cline, V. B., and J. B. Richards. "Accuracy of interpersonal perception—a general trait?" *Journal of Abnormal Social Psychology,* 60, 1960, 1-7.

[4] It should be noted that whatever significance one attaches to the present criterion variables in regard to the various objectives of counseling, the fact remains that it *was* possible to predict some relatively complex and interesting behavior by means of these constructs and projective techniques with greater success than is characteristic of trait-factor-inventory approaches. Although these findings require a good deal of further investigation, this fact is of relevance to the perennial problem of developing adequate techniques of personality assessment.

Dickenson, W. A., and C. B. Truax. "Group counseling with college underachievers," *Personnel and Guidance Journal*, 45, 1966, 243-253.

Erikson, E. *Identity and the Life Cycle*. New York: International University Press, 1959.

Eysenck, H. J. "The effects of psychotherapy," in H. J. Eysenck (ed.). *Handbook of Abnormal Psychology*. New York: Basic Books, 1960, 697-725.

Farber, I. E. "The things people say to themselves," *American Psychologist*, 18, 1963, 185-197.

Gilbreath, S. H. "Group counseling with male underachieving college volunteers," *Personnel and Guidance Journal*, 45, 1967, 469-476.

Krutch, J. W. "Calipers on the human mind," *Saturday Review*, June 19, 1965, 22-25.

Lesser, W. M. "The relationship between counseling progress and empathic understanding," *Journal of Counseling Psychology*, 8, 1961, 330-336.

Luft, J. "Some relationships between clinical specialization and the understanding and prediction of an individual's behavior." Unpublished doctoral dissertation, University of California at Los Angeles, 1950.

Patterson, C. H. "The selection of counselors," J. Whiteley (ed.) in *Research in Counseling: Evaluation and Refocus*. Columbus: Charles E. Merrill Publishing Co., 1968.

Patterson, C. H. *Theories of Counseling and Psychotherapy*. New York: Harper and Row, 1967.

Redl, F. *When We Deal with Children*. New York: Free Press, 1966.

Rogers, C. R. *On Becoming A Person*. Boston: Houghton Mifflin, 1961.

Rogers, C. R. "The necessary and sufficient conditions of therapeutic personality change," *Journal of Consulting Psychology*, 21, 1957, 95-103.

Sarason, S. B., M. Levine, I. I. Goldenberg, D. Cherlin, and E. Bennett. *Psychology in Community Settings: Clinical Educational, Vocational, Social aspects*. New York: Wiley, 1966.

Sarbin, T. R., R. Taft, and D. E. Bailey. *Clinical Inference and Cognitive Theory*. New York: Holt, Rinehart, and Winston, 1960.

Soskin, W. F. "Bias in the postdiction of projective tests," *Journal of Abnormal Social Psychology*, 49, 1954, 69-74.

Taft, R. "Some correlates of the ability to make accurate social judgments." Unpublished Doctoral Dissertation, University of California, 1950.

Taft, R. "The ability to judge people." *Psychological Bulletin*, 52, 1955, 1-28.

Tillich, P. *The Courage To Be*, New Haven: Yale University, 1952.

Truax, C. B. "Personality changes in group psychotherapy," *Journal of Clinical Psychology*, 12, 1966, 221-229.

Volsky, T., Jr., T. M. Magoon, W. T. Norman, and D. P. Hoyt. *The Outcomes of Counseling and Psychotherapy*. Minneapolis: University of Minnesota, 1965.

Vosbeck, Phyllis D. "An exploratory study of the effects of counseling." Unpublished master's thesis, University of Minnesota, 1959.

APPENDICES

Appendix A

Teacher Rating Scale

I. *Personal Cognitive Characteristics*

A. Intellectual Process

1	2	3	4	5
Flexible			**Rigid**	

Ideas and language appropriate to age and ability level of pupils and subject matter.

Teaches at an abstract level of language; ideas too advanced for pupils. A significant proportion of pupils do not appear to understand what intern is saying. Intern not sensitive to ambiguous meaning of own language.

B. Behavior under Stress

1	2	3	4	5
Flexible			**Rigid**	

Stress and anxiety do not drastically narrow the perceptual field. Intern remains "open"—sees what is going on and can report the range of behavior in the class.

Under stress, the perceptual field is narrowed—intern erects a perceptual screen between herself and class—little differentiation; misses pupils' inattention and contributions. Inability to focus on individual and group at the same time.

C. Perspective of Self

1	2	3	4	5
Flexible			**Rigid**	

Proper perspective of self is maintained; can use humor and other devices to look beyond the immediacy of a situation. Perceives what she is doing in class, suggests new strategies, and makes good use of supervisors' suggestions.

Cannot see self or situation in perspective. Intern makes excuses, is on defensive, may blame disinterested pupils or poor direction by supervisor. In the extreme, intern considers giving up teaching.

D. Anxiety and Planning

1	2	3	4	5

Flexible	Rigid
Anxiety provides a spur to increased purposeful effort; concern for planning and a consideration of alternate ways to communicate content and/or relate to pupils. Can plan for the unexpected.	Anxiety inhibits cognitive process, poor lesson plan and time, gets trapped in digressions, cannot handle the unexpected.

E. Overall Rating for Intellectual Process—Manner and Cognitive Style in Dealing with Teaching

1	2	3	4	5

Flexible	Rigid
Optimal use of intellect. Plans, ideas, and language used are functional to pupil learning.	Overly theoretic approach in general. Intern overintellectualizes planning, teaching, and contacts with pupils.

F. Comments on Intellectual Process:

II. *Cognitive Attitude Toward the Pupil*

A. Responsiveness

1	2	3	4	5

Flexible	Rigid
Intern is responsive to the class; sees, listens, and responds to discipline problems, inattention, learning difficulties, students' need for new knowledge and creativity.	Intern does not register "cues"; children's problems are tuned out. Calls on bright students too often and doesn't recognize when to call on the slow child.

B. Attitude

1	2	3	4	5

Flexible	Rigid
Intern views pupil as a partner in educational process.	Intern looks down on pupil; patronizes pupil intellectually.

C. Judgments

1	2	3	4	5

Flexible   **Rigid**

Intern withholds judgments about pupils' ability and performance until she has adequate evidence. Uses a balance of positive rewards and constructive criticism.

Intern makes quick judgments and is unlikely to look for contradictory evidence. May tend to employ negative criticism; picks the pupils' answers apart.

D. Overall Rating for Cognitive Attitude Toward the Pupil as a Person

1	2	3	4	5

Flexible   **Rigid**

Intern recognizes important signals from the class, sees pupil as having a substantive role, makes judgments carefully.

Intern is not sensitive to feedback, looks down on the pupil, and makes snap and categorical judgments.

E. Comments on Responsiveness:

III. *Cognitive Attitude Toward the Communication of Subject Matter*

A. Use of Lesson Plan

1	2	3	4	5

Flexible   **Rigid**

Lesson plan is seen as a vehicle; modification and elaborations are made when and where appropriate.

Literal adherence to lesson plan; sets up what class *must* do. Teaches a lesson plan rather than the pupils. Ignores pertinent related ideas of pupils.

B. Teaching method

1	2	3	4	5

Flexible   **Rigid**

Intern displays a variety of suitable teaching methods, e.g., inductive questioning, dramatization, role playing, projects.

Intern relies on only one or two teaching methods.

C. Teaching Goal

1	2	3	4	5

Flexible   **Rigid**

Teaching for inquiry; interested in means as well as ends; explores where the pupil got off the track. Can flexibly handle unfamiliar content.

Emphasis on ends; assumes a right answer that must be attained the teacher's way. Deals ineffectively with unfamiliar content.

D. Overall Rating for Cognitive Attitude

1	2	3	4	5

Flexible   **Rigid**

Intern uses a variety of methods, flexibility in implementation of plans, and employs inquiry for effective teaching.

Uses few teaching methods, adheres to one or two formats in planning lessons, and employs a prescriptive rather then problematic teaching approach.

E. Comment on Use of Lesson Plan:

Appendix B

Counselor Rating Blank

Supervisor _____

Counselor _____

I. Overall Rating of Competence

1	2	3	4	5	6	7

Extremely effective; works well with clients; approaches "ideal"

Average competence; some shortcomings but generally responsive to clients.

Minimal effectiveness. Goes through the motions.

Negative effectiveness. Does not really listen or understand clients. Preoccupied with himself or irrelevancies.

Comment:

II. Flexibility in the Counseling Process

1	2	3	4	5	6	7

A. Counselor effectively collaborates with clients—explores and examines *with*.

Early closure on presenting problem—little exploration *with* client.

Projective Test Elements:

TAT hero responsive to others. TAT hero sees others as equals. Human Movement (M) responses are equal. Sequence flexible. Variety of content.

TAT hero cuts others out. TAT hero looks down on others. Human Movement (M) responses are condescending. Sequence rigid. Stereotyped content.

Comment:

133

B. Focus on client's perspective.

Gathering information for its own sake.

| 1 | 2 | 3 | 4 | 5 | 6 | 7 |

Projective Test Elements:

M, FM, CF, FC all developed. F% < 60. W, D, record. Takes chances. F+% < 90. Rorschach open-ended.

Corated Rorschach, F% > 60. Obsessive trends, d. Reports facts only, F+% > 90. Rorschach a "Given."

Comment:

C. Flexible responses. Effective repertoires—to feelings, content, and comment on process when appropriate.

Rigid set of responses. Counselor appears straight-jacketed in one mode.

| 1 | 2 | 3 | 4 | 5 | 6 | 7 |

Projective Test Elements:

W++ and W+. Capacity for fantasy. A% < 50. P present but balanced by 0+ and varied concepts. Flexible sequence. Experience balance > 2:2.

Wm. and Wv. No fantasy. A% > 50. P overdeveloped. Stereotyped sequence. Experience balance < 2:2.

Comment:

D. Professionally objective—works within limits of role as counselor.

Overinvolvement with clients (rescue or adoption fantasies) or excessive distance to client—appears reserved—"wooden."

| 1 | 2 | 3 | 4 | 5 | 6 | 7 |

Projective Test Elements:

TAT hero respects integrity of others. TAT heroes consistent in their level of human involvement. Color is F/C and C/F. No hysterical tendencies.

TAT hero overinvolved with others. TAT heroes inconsistent in their level of human involvement. Color is F/C, C/F, C syn. Hysterical tendencies.

Comment:

E. Can handle the unexpected situational contingencies such as outside interruptions or sudden shifts in affect, mood, discussion.

Gets confused in unexpected situations. Seems trapped, appears not to know what to do—flounders.

1	2	3	4	5	6	7

Projective Test Elements:

R developed. F(ch). Shading. W++ and W+. F+% < 90. n low.

R small. Ch. Shading. Wm. and Wv. F+% > 90. n high. Shock. Obsessive defenses. Won't take a chance.

Comment:

F. Interpretation or the suggestion of alternative perceptions, if used, remains close to client's level of awareness—offered tentatively to engage the client's participation and consideration.

Interpretation, appears as an exercise of the counselor's intellectual prowess —attempts to "thread the needle" with extended discussions.

1	2	3	4	5	6	7

Projective Test Results:

F% < 60. F+% < 90. TAT hero sees others as equal. TAT hero responsive to others.

F% > 60. F+% > 90. TAT hero looks down on others. TAT hero cuts others out.

Comment:

III. *Response to Supervision*

A. Listens openly to supervisor. Picks up cues from own tapes. Develops an effective but personally idiosyncratic style.

Appears not to hear supervisor— screens out cues—defends doggedly initial positions. Tries to imitate other styles.

1	2	3	4	5	6	7

Projective Test Elements:

Cooperative response to test situation. Can tolerate ambiguity. Card 4 good form, neutral tone. TAT hero can see self in perspective. Appropriate humor.

Critical, hostile response to test situation. No tolerance for ambiguity. Card 4 hostile base. TAT hero projects. No humor.

Comment:

B. Accurately understands the dynamic complexities of the psychological process within clients, *i.e.,* "normal" problems of developmental

Either naive grasp of dynamics or overintellectual (bookish) labeling of categories. Conveys to supervisor the impression that counseling is either stages—abnormal, long standing disruptive problems. Can convey to supervisor awareness of areas of strength as well as weakness.

"magic" or the classification of clients by "types" or "labels."

| 1 | 2 | 3 | 4 | 5 | 6 | 7 |

Not Rated by Projective Tests

Comment:

C. Consults appropriately with school personnel (teachers and adminstrators).

Provides too much information (gossip) or too little (hides under the cloak of confidentiality to school).

| 1 | 2 | 3 | 4 | 5 | 6 | 7 |

Projective Test Elements:

TAT hero responsive to others. TAT hero sees others as equals. Human Movement (M) interactions are equal. Hero communicates in Sullivan's sense.

TAT hero cuts others out. TAT hero looks down on others. Human Movement (M) interactions are condescending. No communication by hero.

Comment:

D. A professional commitment to counseling as a career emerges. Collaborates well with supervisor. Uses supervision to focus on "self" in role of counselor.

Little commitment or personal involvement in counseling as career—often discusses irrelevant issues in supervision; seems to "miss" appointments; some signs of genuine disinterest; excessive complaints on minor issues of "pollyannaish."

| 1 | 2 | 3 | 4 | 5 | 6 | 7 |

Not Rated by Projective Tests

Comment:

Briefly describe any behavior samples either from supervision or from counseling situations which may add to general evaluation of the counselor.

Appendix B

Rating Manual

COUNSELOR RATING BLANK

Patricia F. Howell and John M. Whiteley

I. *OVERALL RATING OF COMPETENCE:*

This scale is concerned directly with counselor effectiveness. Counselor effectiveness is defined in terms of the ability of the counselor to assist the client in achieving the changes which the client has specified he wishes to make. A counselor is considered effective if the desired goals are achieved, minimally effective if not, and detrimental if his client moves further away from achieving such goals. This scale is concerned with outcome, not technique, with the assumption that we are rating the effects of intervention modes which can be subsumed under the rubric of "counseling." A further assumption is that competence, defined in terms of client change, will be a reflection of a appropriate application of flexibility in the counselor-client interaction and counselor growth as a result of supervision.

In rating counselor competence, the most accurate method would be a pre-counseling and post-counseling assessment of the client on dimensions relevant to the goals of counseling. Lacking that basis for judgment, the supervisor may make inferences about client change based on what the client says in the tapes which the supervisor assesses, collaborated by what information apart from the tapes may be available from school personnel, the counselor, or school records.

Inter-Rater Agreement in the Use of the Counselor Rating Blank Manual

The first assessment of inter-rater agreement in the use of the Counselor Rating Blank Manual is provided by evaluating the size of the discrepancies between three raters after they listened to ten tape recorded counseling sessions, each of 50 minutes duration. The results from this assessment are presented in Table 1.

Appendix B

Table 1

Per Cent of Agreement and Size of the Discrepancies in the Evaluation of Counselor Behavior from Tape Recordings (70 judgments per rater)

Number of Scale Points of Discrepancy*

	0	1	2	3	4	5	6
Ra vs Rb	18	30	31	16	4	1	0
Ra vs Rc	17	43	26	13	0	1	0
Rb vs Rc	27	39	20	14	0	0	0

* The range is from 0 (Complete Agreement) to 6 (Complete Disagreement). Per Cent of Agreement and Size of Discrepancies in rating the seven point flexibility scales of the Counselor Rating Blank between Rater A (Ra), Rater B (Rb), and Rater C (Rc). All raters were doctoral candidates in Counseling Psychology.

Another method of presenting the inter-rater agreement is a correlation analysis between the ratings of two raters (Rd and Rc) on the flexibility dimensions of the Counselor Rating Blank. The results from this analysis are presented below in Table 2.

Table 2

Correlational Analysis between Two Raters (70 judgments) of Ratings Using the Counselor Rating Blank.

	I	IIa	IIb	IIc	IId	IIe	IIf
Rd vs Re	.70	.60	.51	.32	.60	.66	.57

These raters shared the following characteristics:
1) Both were doctoral candidates in counseling psychology.
2) They had no previous knowledge of the Counselor Rating Blank or the Manual.
3) They did not know any of the subjects so their ratings were not contaminated by any other source of information than the tape recorded counseling sessions.

I. COMPETENCE

Rating 1:

The goals determined by the client are achieved the majority of the time and almost always are approached. Client change is seen as the result of the counseling intervention and may include by-products such as greater client satisfaction with himself, personal ease, increased ability to relate to others, increased efficiency and goal-determined behavior, less concern with self, and lessened anxiety. Counselor behavior is professionally appropriate and effective, as inferred from client change.

Rating 2:

The same specification holds as in Rating 1 above, but is achieved with less regularity and less systemization. Goals for counseling are achieved but the relationship between counselor intervention and client change is not as apparent.

Rating 3:

The counselor is markedly successful with many clients and not so with others. Professional behavior is appropriate. Counselor is conscientious, but not consistently successful.

Rating 4:

The counselor is neither outstandingly successful nor consistently failing. The counselor is often quite competent, yet lacking in effectiveness at other times. The relationship between counselor behavior and client change is not too apparent.

Rating 5:

The counselor is generally unsuccessful in assisting clients toward achieving their desired goals. Professional behavior lacks appropriateness in some areas. There is minimal client change.

Rating 6:

Clients seem uneffected by the counseling intervention. Outcome is equivocal and change nonexistent. In retrospect, more time was spent by the counselor with his clients than can be justified by the amount of desired change which was achieved. The counselor contributes virtually nothing by his professional involvement.

Rating 7:

Clients would have been better off without contact with this counselor. The counselor may mean well, but his effect on clients is undesirable. Client change, if any, is away from his desired goals. Client change is in the direction of less satisfaction with self, more anxiety, increased feelings of guilt, worthlessness, and apathy. The counselor is a detriment to the profession.

II. FLEXIBILITY IN THE COUNSELING PROCESS
II A. Collaboration

Ratings in the area of collaboration will be illustrated by four examples: a client statement followed by seven possible counselor responses, and three counselor-client interactions rated respectively 1, 4, and 7.

EXAMPLE A—SEVEN COUNSELOR RESPONSES TO CLIENT STATEMENT

Client Statement

So I thought I would go into medicine, but as I said before, there was—there is this great desire in me to be outside of life, part of the time—and I also want to travel. So there are two problems that I had to try and combine with the field of medicine. I thought possibly I could do research work after I get an M.D. and I might travel that way—see something of the world. I feel kind of like I've lived in a sterile environment, protected in a little glass box that my family built and, uh, I feel very deeply there has to be more for me to see. I can learn a lot more by traveling . . . A lot of this stuff sounds corny, but, I really believe it. I can't help it.

Possible Counselor Responses

Rating 1: Right now, you feel pretty confined and boxed in, and just wish you felt more sure as to what you're doing.

Rating 2: You really feel that now you must break out of these patterns you've been caught up in.

Rating 3: You're pretty confused as to how to go about doing what you want to.

Rating 4: So you're interested in medicine more than any other career.

Rating 5: That's what counts.

Rating 6: Well, if you don't bring up your grades, you'll never get into medical school.

Rating 7: By your age, you should be over this loafing-around stuff.

EXAMPLE B—RATING 1

The counselor and client are working together to unravel the client's conflict and to find a more efficient way to deal with the situation which is of concern. The counselor's responses promote continued evaluation by the client of his thoughts and feelings, yet assist in further exploration.

Client 1:   You know, that's where I got this whole idea in my head that . . . that I just have to stick it out and not be a coward . . . But it seems to me that sometimes you reach a point where you're not being a coward anymore—that you've made a decision . . . and you—it turned out to be one that just wasn't a good one so you remake a decision and there's no reason to stick it out. That's a hard—that's a hard kind of thing for me to reconcile because or—that's the way that I'd always felt before.

Counselor 1: There's something way back in your mind that says—even if it's a bad decision—that I have to accept it and live—(interrupted)

Client 2: Yeah.

Counselor 2: with it.

Client 3: That's right.

Counselor 3: And if something comes up that you almost could bet on being a good thing . . . you can't change to that one even though it looks better, because there's more virtue . . . in sticking it out with the other.

Client 4: Yeah, now then, see, that sounds wrong to me now when I think about it, it really does. Because I'm sure that there are cases where you should be able to leave—or be entitled to run . . . or, I'm not really sure about . . . my thinking . . . about this semester, whether I really am entitled now to leave . . . and, of course, there are just about a—there are a thousand implications in this, because I do have to worry about things like courses and stuff. But maybe, you know —well, it sometimes just looks to me like, well, "maybe—maybe you have given it all you can." I admit that I haven't, but . . . I always think . . . in the back of my mind that even if I gave it all I can— it's not here for me.

EXAMPLE C—RATING 4

The counselor attempts to collaborate with the client, but the result is a primary concern with the facts surrounding a third person or thing which is problematic. The counselor is not collaborating with the client on the client's response to the situation in an attempt to develop more effective ways of dealing with it. The counselor does try to work with the client on understanding the problem.

Client 1: And now she doesn't like me any more and she's causing trouble for me so before I get into trouble I thought I should come and see the counselor.

Counselor 1: Ahuh.

Client 2: Here I am.

Counselor 2: Right . . . now see if I understand. This girl and you were close friends at one time?

Client 3: No, not close—I mean you know—we talked.

Counselor 3: But you were friendly with each other in homeroom section?

Client 4: Ahuh.

Counselor 4: And now suddenly—without any cause . . .

Client 5: Well, uh, I didn't do anything wrong.

Counselor 5: Ahuh, and now suddenly she's, ah, doesn't talk with you any more and she's causing some trouble.

Client 6:   Yeah. (Long pause.)

Counselor 6: You don't have any, I mean it just happened, you don't really know why?

Client 7:   I don't know.

Counselor 7: For the change and about the trouble—I mean, can you just tell me a little bit more about it so I get some indication of—(interrupted).

Client 8:   Well, let's see. In homeroom, I usually read or do some work in English.

Counselor 8: Ahuh.

Client 9:   And so, a couple times I had to refuse to help her make these flowers for the Homecoming and . . .

EXAMPLE D—RATING 7

The client and counselor are not working together. The counselor's statements are seemingly without regard for the particular concerns of this client. The client and counselor do not function together toward the same end.

Client 1:   Well, I'll sit there not even thinking about the subject and thinking about somebody else or something else . . .

Counselor 1: See now, if you know yourself better, you might know why you did that, wouldn't you?

Client 2:   Well, what do you expect? Eeh, let's forget about myself—I still don't understand anyway.

Counselor 2: Well, no—we don't want to forget about you because that's why you're here.

Client 3:   I mean, I . . . I don't get the meaning of "seeing yourself."

Counselor 3: Well, you, ahh . . . you keep thinking about it and talking about it, then you will understand. I don't mean think about it every minute, but I mean, keep trying to figure it out 'cause I think you could . . . figure it out (pause). Well, another example would be . . . with ah,—say a boy or a girl didn't get along with their parents and the parents of this boy or girl were fighting all the time and . . .

II B. Focusing

Ratings in the area of focusing will be illustrated by four examples: a client statement followed by seven possible counselor responses, and three counselor-client interactions rated respectively 1, 4, and 7.

EXAMPLE A—SEVEN COUNSELOR RESPONSES TO CLIENT STATEMENT

Client Statement

I don't really know . . . uh, sort of how I feel about it. I do want to give it as much of a chance, you know, as possible. Some of the pressure has let off, with the talk with Mr. Smith. We cut my schedule down to nine credit hours, three courses, you know, which I feel I can really handle well. And I'm not being completely swamped. But I'm kind of hesitant to take, you know, go back to a full load again. But if I improve somewhat—why, I'll feel a little better about it.

Possible Counselor Responses

Rating 1: Are you saying that you really would like to find the best way to bring up your grades, but if you go back now to a full load you'll be swamped?

Rating 2: You'll begin to feel better about your school work if it improves?

Rating 3: You think that if you go back to a full load again, you'll be swamped?

Rating 4: What are you doing now to improve your grades?

Rating 5: What are your grades anyway?

Rating 6: There's no reason why you can't do better than you have been—with only nine hours now.

Rating 7: What brought down your grades in the first place? Too much socializing?

EXAMPLE B—RATING 1

The counselor concerns himself with the client's perspective in order to help the client understand his problems and find a way of handling them.

Client 1: I've heard a lot of people say stuff like, "When you're dealing with yourself, think with your head; and when you're dealing with others, think with your heart," and all these lovely kinds of sentiments and, I mean, it makes good sense to me—it really does. But I don't know whether I have control or dominance or whatever. But again, I'm not quite sure how, if it, can I—well I'm going to ask you again: Can you rationally decide that this is an illogical approach and then rationally decide that you're going to start sharing with people or something? I don't know if this makes sense to you . . .

Counselor 1: Now once again I think I (interrupted)

Client 2: Hear me say—

Counselor 2: Um, you're saying: "I can't rationally decide something and then do it."

Client 3: Yeah.

Counselor 3: "I can rationally decide something, but emotionally, I'm not always with my rational decision."

Client 4: Yeah, right . . . right.

Counselor 4: "I can't go all the way through with it even though it sounds good —what I've figured out . . . but I can't go-through-with-it-all-the-time."

Pause.

Client 5: I guess, though, I'm not totally convinced . . . that maybe I can't. You know, like maybe . . . maybe I can kind of think my way into a new approach, think my way into a sharing relationship . . . like . . . well, see, part of it is, you know, I've looked around and I just haven't found any . . .

EXAMPLE C—RATING 4

The counselor focuses often on extraneous factors which are not specifically relevant to the problem-solving endeavor with the client. The counselor eventually focuses on most of the important factors, but does so indirectly and takes a long while doing it.

Client 1: I have to write this paper on the development of characterology, which I only find one book on and it's a relic, I think, you know, like 1927. I think I'm looking for something—(interrupted)

Counselor 1: Oh, quite old.

Client 2: Now, I really can't find any more, and I've been going to the Med. School, when I get a chance. I think I'll get a chance at dinner time tomorrow and this is the only one I find over there and I think since I did poor (lowers voice) on the test, I think I better do better on this paper which has to be turned in before the fourth and then I—(interrupted)

Counselor 2: Did you get a bibliography for your paper?

Client 3: Well . . . no.

Counselor 3: A list of references you can use?

Client 4: No, I didn't . . . All I did was I took the topic and I went to the files, you know— looked under "characterology" and, well— first I looked under "character," you know. I did, well—in a sense, I got all the books that I could find with just the title . . . Maybe I'm looking for the wrong thing. I think I started all wrong probably.

Counselor 4: It seems you're quite caught up with this paper and are confused about what you're doing.

Client 5: Yes, I think I'm going around in circles, and I'm not getting any place and time is running out—(interrupted)

Counselor 5: Perhaps it would help if you could explain to me just what you're trying to say on this paper.

EXAMPLE D—RATING 7

The counselor's gathering of information seems unwarranted. Information gathered by the counselor is not put to specific use in the later course of counseling.

Counselor 1: What's uh, what, uh, the biggest thing that's bothering you?
Client 1:   The last few weeks?
Counselor 2: Ahuh.
Client 2:   The Prom.
Counselor 3: What's the big deal about the Prom?
Client 3:   Oh, it's just that it's so neat, um . . .
Counselor 4. Huh, what kind of a prom is this?
Client 4:   A football prom.
Counselor 5: A football prom: Is this for the whole school?
Client 5:   Nuh, um—just the freshmen.
Counselor 6: Oh, I see. I guess you're all excited about that?
Client 6:   Yeah.
Counselor 7: Do you have a date and all that?
Client 7:   No, I'm not going.
Counselor 8: You're not going?
Client 8:   No, I haven't been asked.
Counselor 9: Well, how do you feel about that?
Client 9:   Uh, I don't like it. (laughingly)
Counselor 10: What are you going to do about it?
Client 10:   Just keep hoping—that's all you can do.
Counselor 11: Have your friends been sorta excited about it, too?
Client 11:   Yeah, well, those that have been asked . . . and those that haven't
                been asked all want to get asked, and it's a big thing.
Counselor 12: Most of them been asked?
Client 12:   No . . . Well, most of the guys are asking girls from out of school
                and the girls are asking boys from out of school . . .
Counselor 13: Are these—so I guess that keeps you up nights?

II C. Flexible Responses

An effective repertoire of responses cannot by definition be evaluated on the basis of an isolated segment of a particular session. Rather, it is necessary to assess the variety of appropriate approaches which a counselor may use both across sessions with different clients and within a session or sessions with one client.

An assumption in this approach to assessment is that no one counseling strategy is appropriate with all clients, or even with the same client during the entire course of a counseling relationship.

Ratings in the area of flexible responses will be illustrated by four examples: a client statement followed by seven possible counselor responses, and three counselor-client interactions rated respectively 1, 4, and 7.

EXAMPLE A—SEVEN COUNSELOR RESPONSES TO CLIENT STATEMENT

Client Statement

I really felt as though I'd, that my grades would be a lot better this semester ... and I was more optimistic—you know, feeling better, more confident about myself. I thought that I'd be able to do okay ... Then yesterday, when I got the letter saying I'd been put on probation—well, it really shocked me, for one thing ... and last night my concentration was—uuugh ... and I just didn't know what to do then.

Possible Counselor Responses

Rating 1: And it seemed hard to remember then that you had already known that your grades weren't good and you'd worked out a program for getting your work done ... But you reacted as if I'd said to you: "You ought to be scared about your grades!" And you responded: "Okay! Okay! I am scared!"

Rating 2: Getting that letter yesterday just made you worry all over again about your grades. You felt just as bad about them as you did earlier.

Rating 3: Receiving that letter just took away your ability to concentrate on your work.

Rating 4: You just didn't know how to react to that letter.

Rating 5: So you're really worried about it all again.

Rating 6: So you just don't know what to do now about your grades.

Rating 7: So you're back in the same situation with your grades as you were before.

The responses rated 1 and 2 capture both the content and feeling of what the client was trying to communicate. Those rated 6 and 7 merely focus on content. Again, the differential feature is the straight jacketing in one mode.

EXAMPLE B—RATING 1

The counselor's responses are closely tuned to the client's behavior within and outside of the counseling relationship. The counselor's responses are specific to the client in terms of both the content and feeling of the client's verbalization.

Client 1: You know, I just, I look for answers and I really did—I thought I understood what you were talking about ... Maybe I really didn't understand the approach that you were asking me to take. But I thought I had a feel for it, and then I couldn't do it ... I did a lot of thinking ... and I'd really like to get rid of this deal that everybody should, should worship me or something because that's —you know, that's an irrational kind of idea.

Counselor 1: So what you're saying maybe—(interrupted)

Client 2:   Yeah.

Counselor 2: That you almost feel on the one hand that you ought to apologize to me for somehow not understanding what I was saying and you're saying, "Gee whiz—I've tried, and I can't really follow through with what we've talked about . . . I can't do it."

Client 3:   Well, not really, I mean, I just—I know that's not really the way you feel . . . So I mean, I really don't think I feel that way consciously.

Counselor 3: "But I still can't get rid of that notion—(interrupted)

Client 4:   Yeah, I still can't do it . . . It still isn't comfortable, I'm still not coming out strong in that area . . .

EXAMPLE C—RATING 4

The counselor attempts to respond appropriately to the specific verbal behavior of the client, yet his responses often lack perspective because they are too heavily weighted in either the content or feeling mode. The counselor nevertheless earnestly attempts through his responses to communicate meaningfully with the client.

Client 1:   If I go into medicine, I'll always have a desire to be outdoors and, or to be able to see beauty—what I appreciate.

Counselor 1: Oh, I see, uhm—well, how strong, though, is this desire to be outside as opposed to, I mean, how much does it conflict with your desire to go into medicine?

Client 2:   Well, right now, it's the only thing that I want . . . but that's because this, I, well—(interrupted)

Counselor 2: What's the only thing you want?

Client 3:   To, to be . . . (interrupted)

Counselor 3: To be outside?

Client 4:   Yeah,—*to sense*—that's the easiest way to put it. Uh . . . but then, other times, I don't know, maybe it's periodic.

Counselor 4: Well, have you thought about other fields that might get you into the outdoors, any other fields?

Client 5:   Well, I used to envy the sort of person who could be a forest ranger, but it would just bother me. Maybe it's just a reminder of the fact that I'm just another cog in the world or society. I don't want to feel the responsibility of anything to society, I don't feel any affection for it at all.

Counselor 5: Can you explain to me how you want to help society but at the same time you don't want to feel responsible to it?

EXAMPLE D—RATING 7

The counselor's responses are stereotypical and focus exclusively on content. Responses are not made specifically in regard to a particular client or counseling interaction. When a focus on feeling is called for, the counselor cannot make the necessary shift in his manner of responding.

Client 1:   Oh, it hurts my ears . . . because the study hall is not very quiet . . .
                 but most of the time during study hall I go up to the band room
                 and, uh, practice.
Counselor 1:   Oh, I didn't know that.
Client 2:   Yeah.
Counselor 2:   You get a pass from Mr. Brown?
Client 3:   Ahuh.
Counselor 3:   And you practice that hour . . that's nice.
Client 4:   So, I get, uh, most of my practicing done during the day, which ·
                 really helps a lot.
Counselor 4:   It really helps to give you time to study.
Client 5:   Ahuh.
Counselor 5:   OK—well, I was going to offer you passes to the library every day.
Client 6:   Ahuh.
Counselor 6:   And I made them out so we wouldn't have to spend time making
                 them out if you wanted them . . . but I didn't realize that you had
                 the other interest—so I'd like to give them to you just in case you
                 want them.
Client 7:   OK.
Counselor 7:   OK . . . —and what I did on the last one was, I can only give you a
                 week's worth at a time, so at the end of the week, if you'll come up
                 here, I can give you a new batch.
Client 8:   OK.
Counselor 8:   OK?
Client 9:   OK.
Counselor 9:   OK, it's completely up to you, what you do with them.
Client 10:   OK.
Counselor 10:   OK . . . Are you . . . are you down at the band room now?
Client 11:   Ahuh, I'm just practicing.
Counselor 11:   OK.
Client 12:   OK.
Counselor 12:   OK, I'll let you go back to that.
Client 13:   OK.
Counselor 13:   OK.

II D. Objectivity

Ratings in the area of objectivity will be illustrated by four examples a client
statement followed by seven possible counselor responses, and three counselor-client
interactions rated respectively 1, 4, and 7.

*EXAMPLE A—SEVEN COUNSELOR RESPONSES TO CLIENT
STATEMENT*
Client Statement

I found out that your first name is Judy . . . Can I call you that?

Appendix B

Counselor Responses

Rating 1: For some reason you'd like to be able to call me by my first name . . .

Rating 2: Calling me by my first name would be a lot more comfortable for you?

Rating 3: Why is it that you'd like to call me by my first name?

Rating 4: I'm wondering if going on a first name basis is really appropriate for our relationship.

Rating 5: Do you really think that calling me Judy would be right?

Rating 6: Oh, of course you can call me that . . . Call me whatever you wish.

Rating 7: No. You'd better call me Miss Smith as before.

The central feature of the response rated 1 was a focus on the reason why the client wanted to construe the relationship in familiar terms. The response rated 7, however, was an arbitrary imposition of impersonalization without any consideration of the client's feelings.

EXAMPLE B—RATING 1

The counselor defines his role as someone to help the client work out specific issues in his life more satisfactorily. The counselor shows his interest and concern for the client, but is neither motherly nor does he offer the client counseling as a panacea.

Client 1: The reason I came here is that I'm not happy here in school. I'm not doing well, and I don't really know why I'm in school in the first place. My parents tell me that I have to decide soon what I want to do next year—stay in school or leave or whatever—and I just don't know what I really want . . .

Counselor 1: Right now you're pretty unclear as to what you really would like to be doing and feel as though you should make some decisions for the future.

Client 2: Yeah . . . but I just don't know what I want . . . or how to go about finding that out . . . and I came here to get some help from you.

Counselor 2: It seems that there are some areas for you which are pretty confusing now . . . and that you'd like to feel comfortable enough with me to really examine them more closely . . . and I'd like to help you be able to do that.

EXAMPLE C—RATING 4

The counselor is concerned with the client and his problem, but distances himself subtly from the client. The counselor's behavior tends to be wooden and demanding.

Counselor 1: What about music—what do you plan to do with it? Do you plan to try to make a living with it?

Client 1: I'll try . . . I don't know. I mean, I'm not saying it will work . . .

But, uh, I want to play. I want to play music, you know, like at night or something like that.

Counselor 2: Why do you want to play it—just because it makes you feel good?

Client 2: I like it. (in a determined tone)

Counselor 3: You like music . . . How about making some kind of musical career for yourself, as that could be uh . . . (interrupted)

Client 3: We got a pretty good chance to make it . . . you know, when we had that thing downtown at . . .

Counselor 4: Yeah.

Client 4: We made fourth in the city . . . There ain't no way that we ain't got a good chance, you know . . . If you get, I don't know, if you get upward like some bands, you get at $200, $300 a piece every night.

Counselor 5: You could work some place as a music teacher . . .

EXAMPLE D—RATING 7

As an introductory statement in a counseling situation, the counselor induces the client into responding with very personal data. The counselor defines his role loosely and in a manner which fails to describe the appropriate limits of the relationship.

Counselor: I'm interested in knowing about you, and so I'd like you to tell me anything that you, what you're interested in, about your vocational plans or your family, your problems, or whatever happens to strike your mind.

II E. Unexpected Situational Contingencies

Ratings in the area of unexpected situational contingencies will be illustrated by four examples: a client statement followed by seven possible counselor responses, and three counselor-client interactions rated respectively 1, 4, and 7.

EXAMPLE A—SEVEN COUNSELOR RESPONSES TO CLIENT STATEMENT

Client Statement

Well, I don't quite know how to say this—but, after I left the other week, I —well, I heard some of the other counselors in the office here talking . . . Well, it bothers me, because I've said some things to you that I've never said to anyone at all before . . . And, well—I guess I'd better . . . Well, what they said was that you didn't know what you were doing . . . that you're not a good counselor . . .

Possible Counselor Responses:

Rating 1: And that made you feel pretty uncomfortable about our relationship.

Rating 2: Hearing that made you pretty doubtful about working with me.

Rating 3: So you felt bad about having told me some of your private concerns.

Rating 4: You didn't know what to think when you heard that.

Rating 5: What exactly did they say?

Rating 6: Well, do you trust me or them?

Rating 7: Well that's not true at all. I've been in this business for a long time and . . .

EXAMPLE B—RATING 1

When the client starts to cry, the counselor, by being silent, allows the client to regain control and composure. Since the silence of the client is respected, the counselor effectively gives the client the opportunity to work through some of her feelings.

Client 1:   I just haven't worked at all this semester, right from February on. I haven't done any work . . . and I could never get it done now— I don't even want to . . . I hate it here . . . I can't stand it any longer . . . I just have to leave.

Counselor 1: It looks as though you want very much to leave school now.

Client 2:   Yes . . . I hate it. (Starts crying.) (Long pause while the client cries, sobs and stares off into space) . . . I just have to get out of here. (Determinedly)

Counselor 2: Perhaps what we should do here is decide the most efficient way for you to leave school.

Client 3:   Yes . . . (Cries for about five minutes) . . . Should I talk with the Registrar first?

EXAMPLE C—RATING 4

The counselor's reaction to an unexpected intrusion on the counseling session is inconsistent. The counselor at first interrupts the client and attends to the intruding situation, then he returns to the client. The counselor's policy for handling such interruptions is inconsistent, but not badly inappropriate.

Client 1:   . . . That's not the only thing though. I know several seniors here who are really hep on the school and I ask them what they like about it. And they say that maybe it's not ideal for me, but I don't think they're totally aware of what's —(Phone in office rings . . .)

Counselor 1: Wait just a minute, please . . . Hello. Uh, yes. I see . . . right . . . Well, I'm busy at the moment . . . Could I call you back in a half an hour? Okay, Bye . . . Excuse me . . . You were saying that you don't think those people really understand the whole story?

Client 2:   Right . . . I don't think they want the same things as I . . .

EXAMPLE D—RATING 7

When an interruption from outside occurs, the counselor shifts his attention entirely to that. The client's concerns are left hanging, and the counselor does not appear to recognize or appreciate the client's feelings about the interruption. The counselor's rigidity causes uncertainty in the client about the counselor's regard for him.

Client 1:   My mommy and daddy are always fighting and when I get home (a knock on the door is heard) . . . from school at night I always have to do some chores like the garbage or the lawn and I never get to (another knock on the door) . . .

Counselor 1: Come in! . . . Hello . . . What do you want?

Principal 2:   Oh, I'm sorry to disturb you . . . I didn't know that you were busy . . . I can talk with you later.

Counselor 2: No, that's all right. Jimmy was just about to leave . . . and I can see him some other day.

II F. Use of Interpretation

Ratings in the area of use of interpretation will be illustrated by four examples: a client statement followed by seven possible counselor responses, and three counselor-client interactions rated respectively 1, 4, and 7.

EXAMPLE A—SEVEN COUNSELOR RESPONSES TO CLIENT STATEMENT

Client Statement

When I am depressed why, it's uh . . . I just stay depressed, I guess, you know, I get in the habit—the more I think about my problems when I'm depressed, why the more depressed I get, instead of feeling better. And I have these anti-depressants but, you know, but, I really don't want to become dependent upon them, and I see myself doing so because uh . . . when otherwise I really would have been down in the dumps, why they do work . . . I mean I do stay cheery . . . but I just can't see myself taking them forever and ever . . .

Possible Counselor Responses

Rating 1: You sure would like to be able to do something about it yourself. You kind of wish that you didn't have to accept the depression and the medication—be it good or bad as it comes—that you could make a difference yourself.

Rating 2: You feel the need of doing something about your concerns so you can get off the medication.

Rating 3: You're getting tired of feeling cheery from medication and wish you really had a reason to be cheery.

Rating 4: Well, why don't you try it with the medication only occasionally, so you won't feel dependent upon it.

Rating 5: You ought to just try to bring up your grades and then you won't have that to worry about.

Rating 6: What do you really have to be so depressed about in the first place.

Being on academic probation isn't so bad . . . All you need to do is concentrate on your grades and you won't need to be depressed.

Rating 7: The problem now is that you've become dependent on medication, you no longer feel the urgent need to change your life. You've got to nevertheless, if you want to do anything worthwhile as a human being.

EXAMPLE B—RATING 1

Interpretation is employed at a level which is just below the client's verbalizations. Interpretation is not offered as a threat to the client, but more like a clarification of his thoughts. Interpretation is offered more as an hypothesis than a dictum.

Client 1: I haven't been very happy lately with my social life . . .After I broke up with Jim five months ago, I just haven't done any dating . . . I just seem to have a hard time getting to meet new people . . .

Counselor 1: You've wanted to get out and meet new people, but you've been hesitant to do it.

Client 2: Yeah . . . I feel funny going up to someone in a crowd . . . You know, awkward, and I don't know what to say, to ask them . . . or what to say to them about me.

Counselor 2: It's as if you didn't know how to present yourself to someone whom you didn't know.

Client 3: Well, what could I say . . . that would interest someone. I haven't really done exciting things to tell anyone about or anything like that. I don't know who would be interested in me.

Counselor 3: When you meet someone for the first time, it's almost as if you assume that you couldn't be of interest to them—that you don't have anything special to offer.

Client 4: Yeah . . . I figure, what do I have that somebody else doesn't have too?

Counselor 4: You feel you don't have anything special to offer anyone as a friend . . . and this feeling seems to sort of inhibit your behavior socially.

EXAMPLE C—RATING 4

Interpretation is relevant to the concerns of the client, but is offered by the counselor too hastily and authoritatively. Interpretation becomes anxiety-arousing rather than a facilitator of further discussion.

Client 1: All my life I've always felt I had to compete with my older brother . . . He's always been first in his class and a good athlete and popular and all . . . And I've just always felt like nothing by comparison.

Counselor 1: You've always felt inferior.

Client 2:   Yes. I always wanted to be better than him—just even a little bit
              better—even in just one area.
Counselor 2: Because you haven't been better than your brother in any area,
              you always have felt that you're not good enough. And when some-
              one doesn't feel good enough, then it always is harder for them to
              succeed at anything they do.

EXAMPLE D—RATING 7

The counselor's use of interpretation is not directly relevant to the concerns of
the client. Rather than engage the client's participation, the counselor stifles it
with global references in terms which are not comprehensible to the client.

Counselor 1: . . . and the parents of this boy were fighting all the time and this
              worried him so . . . that this boy just couldn't think about his
              studies.
Client 1:   I had a girl friend like, she was like that. She didn't tell anybody
              else, but her dad threatened to kill her mom and she was going
              down to the graves a lot—(interrupted)
Counselor 2: Yes.
Client 2:   She was in here talking to Mr. Green about it.
Counselor 3: Ahuh.
Client 3:   But, she was, you know when you thought about it she started
              sorta crying and she got up in the middle of the night and took a
              knife and uh . . . and she killed her . . . and she said "Don't tell
              nobody." . . . but, that, well, you know, anyway—she did some-
              thing like that but she didn't—(interrupted).
Counselor 4: Well, uh, lots of, uh, boys and girls have a lot of things that might
              worry them a little, and, us—if you worry about something too
              much, then you can't study. Threatening to kill somebody, anyway,
              is an expression of hostility that has generally been repressed for a
              long time.

III. RESPONSE TO SUPERVISION
III A. Development of Style

Rating 1:

The counselor is concerned with the application of theory to counseling. He
reads other theories not taught in practicum, and with the supervisor's help, experiments in other ways to modify clients' behavior. He is able to develop a sound
rationale with regard to counseling techniques and a personal and effective style.

While the supervisor's opinions are sought, he willingly contributes to his own
ideas and questions. He is concerned with aligning his counseling to a consistent
theoretical framework utilizing many different techniques.

The student plays his tapes freely and objectively criticizes their shortcomings, seeking to increase his effectiveness. Supervision is a time of learning, not of rationalization. When the counselor comes into supervision, no time is spent on small talk. The counselor has so many ideas he wants to explore in supervision that he quickly picks up from the week before and moves ahead.

Rating 2:

The counselor initially screens out things from the supervisor, but after an area has been opened up for questioning, he is perceptive in evaluating his mistakes. He is able to criticize himself without being overly self-critical. After the counselor has found it acceptable to be less than perfect, he is able to experiment more openly with style modifications in working toward integrating his counseling with a theoretical rationale.

Initially this counselor may have wanted to evaluate client behavior largely in terms of only one frame of reference. When the supervisor suggests other ways of looking at behavior, the counselor willingly broadens his perspective. In later development he is able to find weaknesses in his tapes which escaped the supervisor.

Rating 3:

The counselor is overtly cooperative, though not open in his collaboration with the supervisor. He produces on tapes what the supervisor wants to hear and pays lip-service to ideas close to the supervisor's frame of reference. While his attitude may not be genuine, his performance is good. The counselor's mind is often closed on a particular issue, though sometimes he thinks it over later and slowly demonstrates an increased openness. He picks up cues well from tapes and often suggests other ways of handling a situation.

Rating 4:

This counselor may be very interested in supervisor's positions and not defensive. He takes theoretical ideas and filters them through his own personality. His counseling style is more intuitive and random than based on theory.

The counselor hems and haws when asked the rationale for a particular counseling strategy, and the links between counseling theory and his practice are obscure. His understanding of dynamics is based on concrete units or events from which he is unable to abstract and analyze with his supervisor on the basis of scientific concepts and constructs.

Anything the supervisor wishes to discuss is acceptable to him, as he never brings in ideas or questions he wants to cover. An idiosyncratic style based on the counselor's feeling that "I'm a nice person and you're a nice person, so let's talk" is enough of a theoretical rationale for his work.

Rating 5:

The counselor is somewhat dogged and resistant in accepting suggestions. He seeks answers to his clients' problems, rather than approaches. The counselor's behavior seems based on the idea that, "It's tragic if I make a mistake and doubly so if my supervisor hears it."

The counselor is so intent upon wanting to establish a relationship with his clients and to be liked by them that he is reluctant to set any limits. Consequently he may have a relationship with his clients, but not a professional relationship. He seems unable to articulate clearly to clients what a counselor is and what a client does. Some clients do seem to respond to him in a way which leads to some counseling-like sessions, but this is only randomly achieved.

Another variation is the counselor who is very eager to learn, but who doesn't seem able to from his own insights. He depends on the supervisor and sees him as the source of all knowledge and wisdom. He comes into supervision and says, "Oh, you're the only one who could help me with this." He quickly goes from one topic to another, trying to ask as many questions and glean as much information from his supervisor as possible, switching topics so quickly that very little discussion transpires. He feels personally responsible for the lives of his clients, thinking that if he could only "make it better," then no sadness would ever befall them. He eagerly responds to the supervisor as he sees himself as highly ineffective and in need of tremendous help.

Rating 6:

The counselor may have cut and dried attitudes which are defended adamantly, though they are slowly refined over the course of supervision. The style of counseling is personally idiosyncratic in that he tries to "teach" clients "proper" values.

The values held by the counselor are typically those accepted in our society, though he feels called upon, as a counselor, to instill them in clients whose behavior is aberrant, according to his standards. Typical values are that one should finish high school and consider going to college, one ought to try to treat his parents nicely, and one ought not solicit sexual advances. The counselor has difficulty allowing his clients to transgress from his own particular value system. He defends these values in supervision and is resistant to letting up on them in his work as a counselor.

When asked to justify a technique, he sees this as a personal attack and tries to undo his involvement. An effective style has not developed, though there are some satisfactory elements in his counseling.

The counselor rigorously defends his blamelessness for any situation which the supervisor questions: "There is nothing I can do about that because this other person made it impossible." He is not able to view his tapes at all objectively, and when the supervisor asks about possible alternative ways of handling a situation, the counselor then proceeds to criticize the field of counseling as a whole. There often are extenuating circumstances why he is not able to do better.

Rating 7:

The counselor is highly defensive and screens out his supervisor. There is a minimal attempt to imitate or experiment with other styles. An idiosyncratically ineffective style is developed. He frequently misses supervisory sessions. He is not willing to bring many counseling tapes. The supervisor's suggestions are never taken and tried, and there seems to be no continuity to the supervisory sessions. The counselor's style seems not to have been affected by his supervision experience. He always presents alibis or reasons why the supervisor's suggestions won't work. Counseling is stiff and formal. No appreciable change is evidenced in his counseling during the course of supervision.

He has no interest in hearing what the supervisor has to say. Supervision is not a learning experience. He defends his point of view as a way of never translating the supervisor's suggestions into action. He doesn't pick up cues from his own tapes. Closure on counseling theory and techniques is manifest by a rigid style that is followed as an act of faith.

The counselor is not concerned with the effectiveness of his work with regard to the service provided the client. He is not willing to listen to his supervisor except when absolutely cornered. A supervisory session is a period of rationalization when the counselor seeks to gain complete control and effectively block out any ideas contrary to his own.

III B. Dynamic Complexities

Rating 1:

This counselor has a very impressive grasp of counseling and personality dynamics and a sensitive understanding of people, all of which he is able to utilize in his work with clients.

In discussing clients with his supervisor, it is clear that each client is seen as individually unique in his personal makeup. The counselor is also able to indicate the ways he and his situation are similar to other persons. The counselor is sensitive to the client's reactions and development within the counseling relationship. He is aware of what factors are appropriate to deal with, how to do so, and at what point it should be done in the counseling relationship. Theoretical understanding is a vital part of his work, adjusted to the uniqueness of each client. Such a counselor utilizes all possible sources of understanding: from the client, from psychological testing measures, from normative data, and from his own intuitive framework in order to help the client work out the problematic areas to his greater satisfaction.

Rating 2:

Psychological terms are not employed, but the counselor shows a sensitive understanding of the client. He can make appropriate inferences about the precipitating and predisposing factors in the clients' behavior and the relative severity of his problems. Prognostic indications are based upon the specific goals and progress of counseling and are done realistically.

In discussing personality dynamics, this counselor is apt to refer to clients as being "anxious," "upset," "jealous," "hurt," "mixed-up," rather than employing more psychologically specific terms. The descriptions, though vague, are sensitive and seemingly accurate, and he is able to relate counseling goals specifically and appropriately to each client.

Rating 3:

Having enough understanding of dynamics to be an effective counselor, he has difficulty discriminating finer shades of differences. He generally understands the interaction between theoretical personality dynamics and those of the client, but tends to communicate them in vague and global terms.

An example of this would be in discussing a tape of a first session with the supervisor in which the counselor attributed his client's silence to hostility. The client had been referred to the counselor by the principal for having been caught cheating in class. In beginning with this client, the counselor immediately started dealing with the hostility he saw in the client. It became apparent, after discussion with the supervisor, that the client's silence was due less to hostility than to his fearfulness from not knowing what to expect from the counselor. While the counselor is generally aware of personality dynamics, he fails initially to translate them into effective counseling.

Rating 4:

The counselor's understanding of dynamics may be good but it is on an intuitive level. With difficult situations the counselor is unable to bring psychological perspectives to bear or communicate them with facility. His framework of understanding tends to be after the fact.

An example is provided by the counselor who went to the classroom to pick up his client. The client asked if he could bring a friend with him into the sessions. The counselor replied that this was his time specifically, and the friend could not join the session. The client then became very angry at the counselor. In discussing this episode with the supervisor, the counselor realized that in this session the client for the first time had displayed some deeper feelings toward the counselor. From that point on, after discussing further plans with the supervisor, the counselor was able to make progress with this client whom he had previously been unable to work with effectively.

Rating 5:

This counselor has an intuitive feel for personality dynamics but descriptive statements about clients are vague and naive. He sees counseling as a panacea though he attempts to become more systematic in his understanding of what works, when, why, and how.

While able to do a satisfactory job assessing clients and problems, he occasionally is quite blind to the dynamics of the counseling interaction. An example is provided by a female counselor's relationship with a pubescent male in which the counselor failed to recognize both transference and counter-transference behaviors. When the dynamics of this "love affair" were pointed out to the counselor, she was able to recognize the steps that were then necessary. Again, the understanding of dynamics occurred after the fact.

Rating 6:

This counselor has a marked tendency toward stilted and over-intellectual labelling of client dynamics. He has more understanding of people, dynamics, personality development, and counseling in the abstract than specific counseling interaction situations. With a dedication to intellectualization for its own sake, he has minimal sensitivity to the client within the counseling process. He is able, however, to develop meaningful counseling relationships with persons for whom such interaction is vital. In terminating these cases, the counselor does so abruptly, with no understanding, and seemingly no concern for the dynamics and effects of such a termination.

Rating 7:

This counselor has no real understanding of clients or counseling dynamics, either in common sense or psychological terms. He doesn't align theory with his work as a counselor.

When asked to assess the prognosis for a client in terms of the counseling intervention, this counselor replies that, "It isn't fair for me to say." He feels that objective assessment impinges on the client and uses this as his rationale for having meager knowledge of such dynamics. He is adamant in not going beyond the content level of the client's behavior.

III C. Consultation within the Setting

Rating 1:

Even in a difficult, poorly structured, and antagonistic setting, this counselor has minimal difficulty with the school personnel and is able to enlist their support effectively. His cooperation is optimal, though he is not subservient to the practices of others when he feels they are unsatisfactory.

Working with teachers, this counselor is able to broaden their understanding of his function as a counselor, helping them to assess other students, not only "Problems," for whom counseling might prove beneficial. In working with the administration, this counselor diplomatically defines his role, then fulfills it skillfully.

Rating 2:

This counselor looks very satisfactory in the eyes of the school and is closely in touch with the faculty and administration, who perceive him as doing a good job. While his consultation is effective, it may lack only his not standing up for the client when he is not served justly by general school policy.

This counselor lacks excellence only when he is unwilling to work outside of and/or change school policy for the occasional student who is done a disservice by standard rules.

Rating 3:

This counselor is popular with school personnel, with whom he cooperates effectively. He does not become angry or submissive in difficult situations, though he is not as willing to take on difficulties as might be desired.

This counselor is fairly effective in working out a rapproachment with school personnel who were initially difficult to work with. He dislikes feeling called upon to do such, however. He is effective, but begrudgingly so, and this is sometimes communicated.

Rating 4:

This counselor consults appropriately and is able to work effectively with most of the school personnel. His effectiveness is marred only by difficulty in dealing with some persons, and he is unable to work around these personal difficulties. He is effective with most situations, however.

Rating 5:

This counselor has a lot of difficulty relating effectively with school personnel. They know little of his specific work, and he does little to clear up channels of communication.

By the end of the year, the administration may still be unable to evaluate his school performance as he has not made them aware to any great extent of his endeavors. He has few difficulties within the school, but the lack of consultation and communication with the other school professionals gives the aura of being clandestine. He provides an example of the cubicle phenomenon—the counselor who stays within his office so much that others in the school don't know what he is up to.

Rating 6:

This counselor tends to provide information to persons for whom such knowledge is inappropriate. In seeking to be thought of as vital and important to the school, this counselor is on occasion gossipy.

While dealing appropriately sometimes, often this counselor seems blindly unaware of the responsibilities of confidential information. His diagnoses are sometimes shared in the teachers' room, in the strictest confidence, of course.

Rating 7:

Consultation initiated by this counselor is poor and sparse. The school may be dissatisfied with his involvement there. There is no indication that the counselor can work effectively within the context of the school.

The counselor may complain frequently to the supervisor about his dissatisfaction at the school. He attributes this difficulty to the mental imbalance of the school personnel, and the supervisor doubts that the school people any longer try to communicate or work with this difficult counselor. If he does occassionally communicate within the school, it is inappropriate.

III D. *Commitment to the Profession*

Rating 1:

This counselor evidences a professional commitment by various ways. He is eager to read supplementary material to increase his counseling proficiency. He brings tapes to supervision which are audible and with which he demonstrates his familiarity, being able to give an overview of the dynamics of the session and locating specific sections of importance. He is open to criticism and works hard to revise his notions of an appropriate professional role for himself. He is enthusiastic about the challenges which the counseling profession offers.

Rating 2:

This counselor is genuinely interested in counseling. There is congruence between his personal and professional self. He learns enthusiastically and is interested in counseling for its potential for service. The difference between Ratings 1 and 2 is only a matter of degree.

Rating 3:

This counselor is interested in the profession but not excited or enthusiastic. He seems to be playing a role as a counselor which is somewhat estranged from his personal self and does not attend with his supervisor to this lack of congruence. His concerns lie with pleasing the supervisor rather than with counseling effectiveness.

Rating 4:

His interests seem to stem from the desire for a professional degree and academic success rather than from a genuine commitment to the profession. This counselor seems willing to bend in any direction to please his supervisor in order to rise on the ladder of success. His commitment to "getting ahead" can be inferred from his behavior, but he is unable to focus on this issue with his supervisor.

Rating 5:

While there is some commitment to counseling as a career, this is not clearly in evidence. Supervision is often a casual gab session. He may miss appointments during the semester and not bother to reschedule them. He is very concerned with himself in the role of a counselor, however, and collaborates, though casually so, with the supervisor on these issues.

Rating 6:

This counselor has a deep concern and questioning of his own effectiveness as a counselor and of counseling as an effective treatment condition. He is philosophically and personally skeptical of himself as a counselor. He has a deep commitment to humanity. In questioning the effectiveness of his counseling, he is meanwhile rejecting rather than committing.

Rating 7:

This person's commitment to counseling has been tenuous and continues only while he remains in search of another profession. He complains continually about personal difficulties with academic and field work situations and does a minimum amount of reading and preparation to achieve a passing grade. He has no plans to work as a counselor, much to the relief of his supervisor.

Appendix C

Group Supervision Report Scale

Directions: Read through each report and determine which of the following categories it best fits. In some cases, more than one category will be applicable. The following rules should help to resolve these difficulties.

1. Scoring is in general based on the highest level a given report reaches. For example, a report may include self-criticism (Cat. 3), but if there is detailed reference to own feelings vis-à-vis client or group (Cat. 1), the score is 1. Likewise, if in the midst of reporting a session and the criticisms and comments of group members (Cat. 4), the student very briefly alludes to being upset in the counseling session by a certain event without elaboration (Cat. 2), 2 as the higher score is merited.

2. The exception to Rule 1 involved Category 5. As will be discovered below, there are two general ways of obtaining a 5-rating. One, by omission is not venturing beyond the factual level in the report, and second, by commission is taking up external factors such as course mechanics, indicating submission to the supervisor as a higher authority.

   By commission, 5 is unique in that it can serve to reduce a higher score. For instance, a student may be self-critical (Cat. 3) and then indicate some hostility toward the group and/or the supervisor (Cat. 5). In this event, unless the 3 is *very* good, very concrete and searching, the score is 5. If the 3 is excellent and/or the 5 quite weak, the rating is 4. In the case of 2 and 5, the rating is 4, unless 5 is gross or 2 is marginal; if so, 5 is scored.

   By omission, 5 is of course a category which is scored only when no other category is applicable.

A Scale for Rating Group Supervision Reports for Psychological Openness

5. Any of the Following:

   a. Report deals with external matters only; a factual account of session; focus on information. No attention to own feelings. No evaluation of self by self

or others or, at most, a reference so vague that it is difficult to tie it to anything specific, a very generalized evaluation.

b. Feelings or opinions re: shortcomings or others; hostility to group or
supervisor.

c. Supervisor placed in authoritative role.

—May present him as someone who must be acquiesced to. Indications of
submission to him under protest.

—Has the answers: references to his superior subtlety or intellectual pene-
tration.

d. Feels imposed upon by group and supervisors—does not show any objectivity to own hostility.

e. Put responsibility for some of own counseling behavior on supervisors,
books, or other authorities.

f. Comments on the mechanics of the course, e.g., worth or lack or worth of
class format. Complaints or brickbats in lieu of concrete discussion of session
and expressions of feeling.

4. Any of the following:

a. Report includes criticism of self by others. *Shortcomings of writer as
others see them.* May defend self vs. criticisms of group, but with no indication of own feeling vis-à-vis criticism.

b. Reports on own learning in terms of general issues, discoveries are in
terms of the generalized counselor, "I learned that counselors should . . ."
rather than "It was clear that I should . . ."

c. Claims to have undergone considerable change in regard to counseling
style or personality without discussion of difficulty involved; too pat.

3. Self-evaluation. Discovery of own shortcomings—with some specifications of
them—or picking up suggestion of group and drawing out specific implications for self.

2. Brief reference to own feelings (a phrase or slightly more) in regard to
counseling session itself or to evaluations of counseling by group, supervisor,
or self.

1. Substantial concern with own attitudes and feelings. Own feelings a central
theme in report. Good deal of specificity and elaboration in regard to them.

Appendix D
Scoring Manual

CASE OF JOHN

A competent response to the Case of John would contain several elements: an evaluation by the counselor of the possible reasons for John's appearance in the counselor's office just before the test, an exploration with the client of his concerns in an attempt to assess the problem, and the communication to the client of the counselor's willingness to collaborate with the client in helping him to solve his problems.

The counselor might try to relate the anxiety to discomfort John had experienced before other exams, and what he had learned about himself through counseling. The counselor might offer to accompany John to the exam, thereby providing reassurance and support. If the brief evaluation indicates that the problem is pressing and other than test anxiety, the counselor might offer to work with John at that time, then assist in arranging another testing time. The key elements are not jumping to conclusions but evaluation, exploration, and collaboration.

What follows are actual responses to the Case of John by counselors-in-training with an assessment of each response and the rating assigned to it on a seven point scale from flexible (one) to rigid (seven). In each case, the counselor was asked to indicate his considerations with John standing in the doorway, and how he might act.

FLEXIBLE RESPONSES TO THE CASE OF JOHN
The following response was given a flexible rating (1):

> "More information about John is certainly warranted. Such data as family background, aspirations of the client, etc., would be helpful.
>
> It is certain that John's present condition is due to the previously discussed problem or to another problem. It is important to know something about how the previous sessions with this client have progressed.
>
> I would certainly try to convey to John the feeling that I was interested in him and his problem and wished to assist him to resolve it. I would probably feel that his present condition was due somewhat to his worries over academic work but this would have to be a hypothesis that would have to be examined in the counseling session."

165

The student indicated that more information is necessary. He indicated that it wasn't clear whether the problem was related to previous discussions or to some other problem. The counselor said he was interested in conveying to the student the feeling that he was interested in him and in his problems and wished to help him resolve them, but that further talk would be necessary to clarify the situation.

A realization of the fact that there was not time for extended counseling was provided by the following answer rated flexible (2):

"There would be no *time* for extended counseling (as this test situation is defined). However, some opportunity for expression on his part of his fears (of the test, or whatever else is on his mind) might be helpful at this time. Also, the counselor might remind him quickly of some test-taking behavior that had been discussed previously as a means to lessening anxiety such as taking time initially to outline his thoughts on an essay question before beginning to write. In other words, the counselor's focus in these few minutes would be on two aspects:

(1) Letting John express his anxiety (in hopes that this catharsis would relieve it).
(2) If John desired this or it seemed helpful under the circumstances, the counselor might give John a brief review of test-taking behavior.

There are several troublesome dimensions to this case:

(1) The boy's self-percept obviously (from information given) is one of inadequacy. Thus, a long-range goal would be to raise his self-percept, but this is a profound problem requiring time.
(2) In order to alleviate anxiety, short-range goals would have to be implemented, *i.e.*: relations with peers, study habits, etiological factors (home life, etc.) investigated.
(3) Thoughts and feelings of counselor would include a desire to help, allow boy to express anxieties, feelings and thoughts about himself (his abilities, disabilities, etc.)".

This counselor perceived the necessity of relating previous discussions to the problem, then focusing constructively on the problem, in the time available. This answer didn't take into account that there might be some other matter than test anxiety. Other than that, it was a very sensitive, competent approach to the problem. The counselor attempted to be supportive in the situation. He also noted some practical difficulties.

Another flexible approach (2) to John's problem is illustrated by the following counselor response:

"I would try to put John at ease. After he has told me his concern about the test, I would talk to him about whether he felt that it might be well that he would take the test, unless the reason for his moist eyes is something other than his being upset because of the exam. If this is the case, then I would try to work with him on the basis of this situation. My thoughts at start would be: Why is John here at class time? What is bothering him to the point of tears? What can I do to help him to feel easy? My feelings would be to get John to see that he should take the mid-term exam. I would feel that I could talk with John so that he maybe would be less upset about the testing, if this is his reason for coming in."

This counselor focused on John mastering his anxiety and taking the test. The counselor also noted that the moist eyes might be due to some cause for concern other than the exam. The counselor noted that if that were the case, he would work with John on the basis of the situation. He kept open to other alternatives, but still worked constructively on the immediate problem.

Some counselors are particularly effective at giving the client the opportunity to state why he is there, and then going on to consider a host of questions that might be related. Such was the response rated flexible (2) of the following counselor:

"After giving him an opportunity to state why he is there I would play it by ear. If I felt he would be able to take the exam without going to pieces I would try to get him to face the difficult task of reality. If I felt he would not be able to take the exam without hysterics, I would notify the teacher of his presence in my office. My thoughts would have many questions: Has some immediate crisis precipitated this? Is he prepared for this test? Is he sick, ill, feverish, excessively tired? Does he need to be forced to face what might be a frightening situation or will facing it be the straw that phases him out? What will be the academic consequences of taking or not taking the exam at this time? Has this situation arisen before? If so, what were the dynamics involved, the outcomes? What is the disciplinary protocol of the school?"

This counselor perceived both the complexity of the situation, the necessity of evaluating John's current state, the reality of the school setting, and the necessity for further examination and collaboration.

Another response evaluated as flexible (3) is the following:

"I think I would be wondering what his concern was—the history exam he was on the way to take, or perhaps some exam he had already taken and was concerned about how well he had already done. Since it was just a few minutes until his history exam, I would assume this was his concern. I think I would also wonder what his purpose was in coming so close to the time for the test. Perhaps he was very concerned about the test and maybe unconsciously hoped to stay and talk about it long enough to be late getting there, and therefore, having to him a valid reason for doing poorly. I would feel that obviously a good relationship had been established because of the fact that I, as the counselor, was the person he was turning to when something was bothering him.

The main thing, I think, that would bother me in this situation would be the time element. If the boy was as distraught as he seems to be, I don't think you would give him the help he needed in the two minutes before he was due at his history test."

The counselor sized up the situation by noting that John was on the way to an exam. The counselor wondered what his purpose was in coming. He noted the problem of a time element, and that he couldn't give the kind of help the boy needed just before an exam. This response lacks the detailed considerations about exploration with the client and the offer of collaboration present in the responses rated as most flexible (1).

Another example of a flexible response (3) is provided by the following:

"John appears to be upset and concerned about something because he is tearing up. He hesitates in the doorway which indicates that he is reluctant either to talk about his problem or fearful of becoming emotionally upset in the presence of another person. Because of the time period and the past sessions, one might assume it concerns his scholastic work, testing, etc. However, one should approach John in such a way that he is able to express his feelings without predetermined assumptions or conclusions. One should attempt to show John that he is understood and that he has freedom of expression. Then, the counselor should attempt to make him feel more comfortable and thus to provide John with an opportunity to investigate his situation and perhaps find a solution."

This counselor evaluates the situation as best he can, noting the student is "reluctant to talk about his problem" or "fearful of becoming emotionally upset." The counselor goes on to take into account the situation and says it is possible to assume that "it concerns his scholastic work, testing, etc." A key element in the scoring decision is the following sentence: "However, one should approach John in such a way that he is able to express his feeling without predetermined assumptions or conclusions." This indicates that the counselor sees the need for further examination and collaboration. The answer would have been better had the counselor confronted what to do about the immediate problem of the test.

The following example was evaluated as flexible (3):

"I would wait for him to speak, since he obviously is almost ready to, then go from there. The problem may have to do with exams, as would be expected from the previous resume; but it might not. I wouldn't want to jump to any conclusions. Since I would know him well, I would find it easier to react than just from the resume. My first thought presently is that he is upset over a midterm and how he will do on it. I feel that I want to hear from him what the problem is. It certainly seems imperative to talk to him immediately. Nothing seems particularly troublesome at this point. A lot again would depend on what he says.''

This departs from the ideal in that the counselor assumed that it seemed ''imperative to talk with him immediately.'' However, he didn't jump to conclusions, and notes that, ''a lot again would depend on what he says.'' This counselor did not relate client behavior to previous interviews, nor did he comment on working in an educational setting.

The following example is a very sensitive portrayal of John and his problems, though the counselor does not consider sufficiently the setting and his previous work with the client.

''My first thoughts and feelings would be 'he is distressed and how can I help him?' I would think of the recent sessions we had had, of the test coming up, and wondering if the two were connected. I can't think that I would find any dimension troublesome, but I would feel that I would hope he could get the feelings out about whatever it was that may have been producing the apparent anxiety and concern. This might mean a postponement of his taking the exam at that time; but the important thing would be to reach his perceptions of the situation. The mechanics of late test taking could be worked out later. I would also be aware of the *effort* it may have taken for this conscientious, academically minded young man to come in with these kinds of feelings at this time. From this one might assume two things: (1) he is terribly troubled; and (2) he needs support and unconditional regard.''

The counselor looks very much within the client's frame of reference. He wanted to help the client express his feelings. While he thought that this might mean a postponement of the exam, the important thing for this counselor was to reach the client's perceptions. The counselor recognized the effort it must have taken the client to come. Working within a school setting, the counselor might have been a little more concerned with the realities of the school situation and the possibility of talking him into the test. The counselor also failed to draw an explicit relationship between the recent counseling sessions and the current situation, though he wondered if they were connected. The rating assigned to this answer was three (3).

RIGID RESPONSES TO THE CASE OF JOHN

An example of a rigid answer (5) is the following:

"He thinks he is going to fail the midterm exam. He is very tense, anxious, and nervous. How can I make him feel more comfortable? How can I help him to feel more selfconfident? He just feels he can't go take that exam for fear he'll fail. He seems to try very hard but has no self-confidence. Is he being pushed hard by parents? Is he being pushed beyond his ability? How can I help him to find a way to be successful—build up his positive attitude?"

The counselor evaluates the student as being tense, anxious and nervous. He raises some questions which may need to be explored in the future, then wonders about methods for helping the client achieve certain goals, though it is not clear whose goals. Lost in these counselor ruminations is any constructive immediate action. He also raises questions he should have learned the answers to during the previous sessions, if the questions are deemed worthy of answering.

An example of a rigid (5) response is the following:

"Knowing John's previous apprehensions concerning his academic work, my first impression, as the counselor, would be that he is concerned about passing the history exam. He is studious, conscientious, but always doubtful as to whether or not he has studied enough or will retain what he has learned. What is the basis for his doubts? Is there pressure from his parents, or teachers who expect more of him than he is capable of producing? Is he an over-achiever? Is there something in his background or personal history to make him apprehensive? During the interviews he expresses great concern about achieving as well as his family who are persons of stature in the community. His father is a graduate of Yale and his mother from Radcliff and the two of them are expecting great things from John. Are they expecting too much?"

This counselor makes some statements about the client, then raises some questions about the basis of John's doubts. He then launches into a paragraph talking about what happened in their interviews. This was unrelated to the task. While what happened in their interviews may indeed be germaine to the problem, the counselor did not indicate how. Neither did he consider the situation of their encounter, nor what he might try to accomplish at the time.

An example of a rigid (6) response to the Case of John is provided by the following:

"We do not know how justified John is in worrying about his academic work. Is he really not passing or is he not achieving up to his own or a parental standard? The approach of the counselor would be vastly different. If he is trying and not passing, some study skill techniques seem to be in order.

However, I feel that he may be like a counselee of mine who ranks 34 out of 1128 and is still dissatisfied. She says she knows others who are "8" out of "13." I am trying to get this girl to see that knowledge and a grade are two entirely different items. She ranks in the 98th and 99th percentiles on achievement tests and I want her to feel great satisfaction from this. John seems somewhat similar, however, he may have impossible goals set for him by himself or by others. He seems to be near a cracking point and I would suggest that he postpone the test temporarily until we could talk again over just what place the history grade has in our life ten years from this date."

This counselor began by wondering how justified John is in worrying about his academic work. This seems to indicate that the counselor's approach would be different depending on the degree of "justification." The counselor then immediately says, based on having little information, that John is just like another client he had. The counselor jumps to the conclusion that John may have an "impossible goal set for him by himself or others." On the basis of this shaky conclusion, the counselor suggests that possibly "he postpone the test temporarily." This answer is unrelated to the previous counseling work with the client. It seems to be more related to another case the counselor had than to the Case of John.

The several different elements in a rigid (6) answer are illustrated by the following counselor response:

"You seem to be having great concern over your exam. It appears that you are perpetuating the same behavior which we discussed previously as the cause of this worry. You are saying that if you don't get a perfect grade on this exam you are not worth a damn. This is not so, as we pointed up via many examples. How about it? This concern is over and above what is necessary for the situation. Why don't you try and think about the real results which could occur rather than your perfectionistic goals. By doing this you may be able to go over and take the exam.

I would primarily want to get him to utilize the previous discussions in his action. To get him to take this exam would, if he did well, help him to realize that his concern is really too great and that he is making too much of it. If it worked on this occasion it would be proof of this fact. This would be my first aim. I would also have fears that he might be too anxious to achieve thereby causing him to really feel anxious. Quick action is necessary though not quick enough to make him feel rejected or rebuffed."

The counselor begins by telling John what his problem is, like "It appears to me . . . ." The counselor then tells John what he is saying to himself rather than asking him. The tone is of the lecturer's role, not the counselor's role. The counselor goes on to relate the current situation to previous discussions, which is a reasonable second step, provided the first step is to see if there may be some other problem. The counselor appropriately notes that quick action is necessary, provided the student doesn't feel rejected. What this counselor failed to do was be sufficiently open to examination and exploration. He immediately closed on the presenting problem.

An example of a rigid response (7) is the following counselor's statement, in which his first thought is that his client is worked up over the history test and that he wants to take refuge in the counselor's office.

> "My first thought is that he has gotten himself worked up over the history test and is frightened too much to take it. He seems to want to take refuge in the counselor's offce. The most troublesome part of the situation is whether to allow him to spend any great amount of time in my office. If he stays, I have allowed him to escape facing a difficult situation and this is not a good thing for him to learn, not counting the difficulties he will encounter with a make-up test, the teacher, other students, etc. However, he probably would fail the test and be embarrassed in front of the other students if they noticed his reaction. Another troublesome aspect is my wondering how he could be under such tension and wanting to do something immediately. If he has come in over some other incident, (which he will tell me after coming in) I would be bothered that we hadn't discussed it before."

After jumping to the conclusion that the client seems to want to "take refuge" in the counselor's office, the counselor devotes much of the remainder of his response to debating with himself about whether or not to allow the client to do this. There is an early focus on what appears to be the presenting problem without examination or apparent collaboration.

An example of a rigid (7) response to the Case of John is the following:

> "I wouldn't worry so much about the fact that he was missing the test because he obviously is in no condition to take the test. My concern would be in helping him to release some of the feelings that had built up, so that we could look then at the problem with less emotion. Putting him at ease would be most important and communicating to him that all is not lost."

This counselor immediately jumped to the conclusion that he wouldn't worry that the client was missing the exam because the client was in no condition to take it. He went well beyond the information available. Putting the client at ease is important and humane. Communicating to him that all is not lost is important. What this counselor failed to do was keep an open mind about the nature of the problem, and explore the client's feelings a little more within the several minutes he had. He did not use the information available from the previous counseling sessions, particularly that John usually becomes very upset about exams. This counselor did not remain open to the possibility that the difficulty was unrelated to the examination.

Appendix E
Scoring Manual

CASE OF DAVID

Scoring for the Case of David is on several different dimensions. One dimension is whether the role of the counselor is explicitly defined, implicitly defined, or left undefined. Another dimension is the specific counselor response to the father's question: whether the counselor recognized the contingencies, options, or possibilities open to David. A third dimension on which evaluation is made is the consistency of the counselor's response. The rater assesses whether the counselor specified mutually exclusive or incompatible elements within his answer. The final dimension is the value question: whether the student is seen as an individual, or whether the society's or institutions' values are imposed upon the student.

The raters were asked to make their evaluations in terms of the following format:

I. Role of Counselor

Explicitly defined			Implicitly defined			Undefined
1	2	3	4	5	6	7

II. Specific Response to Father's Question in Terms of Contingencies, Options, or Possibilities

Flexible					Rigid	
1	2	3	4	5	6	7

III. Consistency of Response

Flexible					Rigid	
1	2	3	4	5	6	7

IV. Value Orientation

Student as Individual					Institution-Society	
1	2	3	4	5	6	7

In translating the rater evaluations into assessments of the counselor who wrote the story, four categories were used: Counselor role (I as evaluated), flexibility

(Summation of II, specific responses; and III, consistency), value orientation (IV as evaluated), and overall competence (Summation of I, II, III, and IV, as evaluated).

In this system of tabulation, the ideally competent counselor would have earned a rating of four with an explicitly defined role, a flexible explication of contingencies, a consistent answer, and a value orientation toward the student as an individual.

The totally incompetent counselor would have earned a rating of 28 with an undefined counselor role, a rigidly prescribed response to the father with no options, an inconsistent response, and a value orientation toward the institution and society as paramount.

In presenting examples as guidelines for scoring, an evaluation of the counselor's response will be made with appropriate scoring decisions indicated.

The following answer to the Case of David provides an illustration of each of the dimensions to be evaluated:

> "I would tell the father, first of all, that I do not know enough about the son's situation to say what I think would be the wisest course. Second, I would tell him that this is not a decision I can make for David but that he must make it himself. I would carefully tell the father that I am going to see David again on Monday but again stress the fact that even after that I will not say, Yes David should withdraw, or No, David should not withdraw. Again, this must be David's decision.

> This situation could involve value questions at many different points. First, they would certainly come up in your session with David—how do you react to a boy who wants to withdraw? Certainly the father's values will come into play—does he really want the boy to withdraw or will he insist he stay "because everyone needs college."

> If in talking with the father, you told him, 'no David should not withdraw because he is a capable student, and, therefore, ought to stay in school,' then the counselor would be imposing his own values on the situation.

> I think I am representing not my own values in the sense that David should stay in school but my own values in the sense that I feel a boy this age should not be pushed one way or the other but should be allowed his own decisions and my own value judgment comes in by feeling a person is able to make this decision."

The counselor begins by saying he doesn't know what would be the wisest course. He defines the role of the counselor as being one where the decision is "not a decision that I can make for David, but one that he must make himself." The counselor then presents himself as someone who is going to be working with David and is going to be with him again on Monday.

This answer is weak in that it doesn't spell out for the father any options which might be open to David like dropping a course or two, getting special tutoring help, seeing the instructors to get an inventory of where he is behind, or dropping a science course and adding another course if it's not too late. The response is reasonably consistent. The counselor has presented himself in a role and follows it throughout. The values of seeing a student as an individual are very consistent with the definition of the counselor role. Scoring: *Role*, 3; *Options*, 6; *Consistency*, 2; and *Values*, 3.

In the following approach to the Case of David, the counselor spells out some options in the first part of his reply, but then goes on to practically assume responsibility for the decision with the second point. He concludes by saying that the decision should be left up to the client.

Outline briefly the main points of your reply:

(1) Since the client seems to be overloaded with science requirements, it would probably be best to have him drop one or two but not all of the courses. It seems possible that he might be able to catch up with a few of the courses although not all of them.
(2) The counselor should not give the father a flat decision at this point because he needs more time to think about the matter and more time to discuss the matter with the client.
(3) Also, I feel that this problem should be discussed with the client rather than with the client's father. The client is capable of handling certain problems but has shown that he needs help from the counselor, consequently, I feel that the final decision should be left up to the client.

In what way might this kind of situation bring the value question into focus? What values are you representing in framing your reply to the student's father?

The client is a responsible person capable of making decisions and of seeking help if it is needed.

This person was rated low on every item because the answer was inconsistent, the options weren't really spelled out, the counselor's role was left undefined, and the value orientation was so sparsely defined as to be unclear, except that the counselor was really involved in the decision making process. Scoring: *Role*, 6; *Options*, 6; *Consistency*, 7; and *Values*, 6.

An alternate approach to evaluating the Case of David is provided by the following:

(1) I would hesitate to flatly recommend either dropping or staying at this point. I might know more after the Monday session. It seems unlikely that it is purely the academic load which is the problem.

(2) I would try to prepare the father in the event withdrawal did seem the answer at a later date. One could say that it was better to withdraw rather than flunk out. Some colleges will re-accept students after withdrawal but not after a semester of failure.

(3) It might be that a semester of limited or no academic activity might be the proper therapy for this student, although I lean to the view that this is not a purely academic problem.

This might focus attention particularly on the values the parents hold dear—success(monetary) in life; what the neighbors think, etc.

This also tests the counselor's values—does the client have the right and the ability to decide his own fate? I feel he does but to reiterate—this is not necessarily an academic problem.

This person listed three main points in his reply. The counselor would know more after the Monday session indicating that he's the locus of responsibility, or at least he's deeply involved in the responsibility. The counselor's role here is really left pretty undefined for the father. The counselor could appear to be a Dean for all the explicitness in counselor role that was provided here.

The counselor did try to spell out some possibilities, and prepare the father for alternatives. It is on the value question that this counselor is particularly poor. The counselor first says the focus in the conversation will be on values the father holds dear. Then the counselor's values are spelled out as to whether the client has the right or ability to decide his own fate. The counselor then equivocates by saying that this is not necessarily an academic problem and leaves the value question unresolved, but by default toward the family's values. Scoring: *Role*, 6; *Options*, 4; *Consistency*, 7; and *Values*, 7.

In the following response, the counselor again indicates that he could give an answer if he knew more.

"I would reply that since I'd had only one session with the son, I would be unable to give a definite answer. I think I should talk more with David. If the father wants to sit in on the session, he may, if David agrees with it.

David indicated he'd like to try to work the problem out himself.

David has done very well the first two years, so maybe he can work it out so he won't have to withdraw, unless this is his sincere desire.

The student has the potential to work out his own problem. He should not be pushed one way or the other by the father."

The options are not well spelled out in this case. It is only in the value orientation that there is a tentative move toward the son by saying he should not be "pushed" one way or another. The counselor has left his role undefined. There is an inconsistency in first saying that, "I would be unable to give a definite answer," then saying that, "the student has the potential to work out his own problem." Scoring: *Role,* 7; *Options,* 7; *Consistency,* 7; and *Values,* 3.

In the following example, the counselor has spelled out the value dimension quite articulately. He has indicated that the locus of responsibility is not the counselor's.

(1) The decision of withdrawal is not my decision.
(2) David has hinted at withdrawal, but he has not thought out the situation.
(3) It is necessary that David and I discuss the situation.
(4) What are your feelings about the situations?

If the counselor answers the father's question with a direct reply, the counselor is making a value judgment. The decision must be made by David. If the reply indicates the necessity for further consideration and discussion with David, the counselor is using or adhering to the fact that David as a person is capable of making his own decisions. The value involved is related to 'man as a rational person is capable of arriving at his own decisions.' This same value is included in part by asking for the father's feelings. It also implies that the father as a parent may be able to assist in accepting the boy's situation.

The reply is meant to concentrate on the client's feelings about the situation and not the counselor's.

The counselor appropriately says that he and David need to talk more, then directs the discussion back to the father. This is undoubtedly good counseling strategy. On the other hand, the counselor has failed to clearly define his role or spell out the options open to David. Scoring: *Role,* 5; *Options,* 7; *Consistency,* 2; and *Values,* 2.

In the following example, the counselor has left the counselor role undefined.

"The first main point would be that it is virtually impossible to answer such a question at this time. It would seem that his son is having definite problems as far as academic work is concerned, but this is not to say that it means immediate dismissal. More information would have to be forthcoming from the client before any such decision was made. Also, how does the father feel about it?"

Is there a possibility that something else (besides grades) could be bothering the student? As far as the father knew, the main points would be:
(1) Assess the academic situation; (2) Attempt to ascertain what was
causing it; (3) What could be done about it, *if* the student wished to remain in school.''

"Client-centeredness seems to be the chief value. Does the student
wish to remain in school or doesn't he? If not, why not? I probably
would *feel* a bias regarding the student's remaining in school, but I
would hope I would not impose this on the student. An attempt is
made to look at what might be going on behind the 'grade screen.' ''

The counselor notes that a decision can't be made at this time, though he
acknowledges that the son is having difficulty. He directs the questions toward
the father's feelings, which is probably sound strategy. He tries to spell out some
things that need to be done. In the value question, the counselor notes that he
feels he has a bias but he would not impose it upon the student. Scoring: *Role*,
6; *Options*, 6; *Consistency*, 3; and *Values*, 2.

In the following examples, the counselor has said that pending further sessions,
he would answer "no."

    (1) Pending further sessions, I would answer no.
      (a) His past record indicates it is not an academic problem.
      (b) His presence at the Counseling Service is evidence he does not
         want to drop.
      (c) Therefore, there is every reason to believe that the student can
         salvage some courses (even if some must be sacrificed).
    (2) I would urge further sessions with the student—possibly with the
      father as well.

I represent the belief that education is worth while and should be continued until clear evidence indicates it is hopeless. The values involved
are (a) education (b) the idea of self-reliance, and (c) the assumption
that one person can help another to solve this kind of problem.

The counselor does suggest that the student could salvage some courses. The
student's presence at the Counseling Service however, does not necessarily indicate
that the student doesn't want to drop. His past record indicates that it is not an
academic problem, yet David is taking all science courses which could make it an
academic problem. The counselor urges further sessions but doesn't say why.
Finally in terms of the value question, the counselor can't assign any priorities to
values. The values involved are education, which in a school system would be the
institution-society. The relationship between self-reliance, which would be on the
student as an individual, and the assumption that one person can help another is

unclear. The resulting lack of priorities yields an unclear value position, and by default one toward the institution and society. Scoring: *Role*, 5; *Options*, 6; *Consistency*, 6; and *Values*, 6.

An example of an inconsistent, poorly articulated response is the following:

"I would not give an immediate answer. I definitely feel dropping and stopping isn't the answer by itself.

I would want some background and then further counseling to find out what caused this change in David's previous pattern.

It may be wise to drop one or two courses and catch up in the rest.

One big consideration would be university policy. For example, some schools give failures for any courses dropped after mid-term. This could hurt the boy's record and future school and job possibilities. Another big consideration is the boy (really the main consideration) and what are the causal problems.

It strongly would present the value feelings I have toward a college degree—also David's and his father's. Also all those involved feelings of failure. In my reply I am strongly stressing the importance of David as a person—not only in the immediate situation, but also in the future.

David must make the final decision, but only after consideration of all possibilities and effects."

This counselor first wouldn't give the father an immediate answer. He then felt that dropping out wasn't the answer by itself. He appropriately suggests the need for further background from counseling, and notes the necessary consideration of the reality of the university's policy. Almost as an afterthought, another big consideration is the student.

In discussing the question of values, the counselor said he strongly would present the value feelings he has toward a college degree, but also David's values, and the father's values. Again, almost as an afterthought, he indicates that David must make the final decision. What the counselor didn't do was spell out options to the father, explicitly define the counselor's role, be consistent in the response, or take a consistent stand on the value question. Scoring: *Role*, 6; *Options*, 5; *Consistency*, 6; and *Values*, 6.

An example of a competent response is the following:

(1) The main point of my reply would be to let the father know that while I appreciated his concern, I thought that this was a matter which would require my seeing his son further and a decision which his son

would, at least from my point of view, have to arrive at on his own
after a thorough consideration of the matter.

(2) I would also point out that dropping out was not the only alternative. Certain courses could be dropped if this would be more acceptable
or useful to the boy.

(3) I would try to point out that while the matter of where to turn
academically was important—it would be worthwhile to see if the boy's
piling up of his science requirements was the sole cause of his difficulty,
and if so, to look at his reasons for it or look at any other concerns the
boy had.

(4) I would try to make sure that the father felt that his interest was
appreciated, while making it clear that my role was in large measure to
work with the boy. (I would want the father's interest to be helpful
but not interferring.)

This situation might bring the value question into focus in several ways.

In framing my reply I would be representing client-centered values in
regard to the boy.

I would also try to represent the role of the counselor in a way that
would engage the most cooperation from the family while maintaining
client-centeredness.

This counselor explicitly defined the role of the counselor as working with the
student. The counselor noted the necessity of gaining the cooperation of the family, yet at the same time emphasizing that the student would make the decision
after a thorough consideration of the matter. He noted that there are other alternatives to dropping out, that university policy would need to be considered,
and that science requirements might not have been the sole cause of the difficulty. It is necessary to find other sources. The counselor's response was internally
consistent. The values which the counselor talked about were centered in the
student, and also consistent with the rest of the reply. Scoring: *Role,* 1; *Options,*
2; *Consistency,* 1; and *Values,* 1.

Another response to the Case of David is the following:

"I would ask him how he felt. If he insisted in asking my opinion out-
right, I would tell him that the decision was not mine, but his and
his son's. I would tactfully then explain that this semester's failing work
goes beyond a mere cramming of science courses into one semester and
that perhaps David had some other concerns which he needed to discuss and work out. Then I would list the alternatives facing them now

which are withdrawal, staying, dropping two or more courses and planning to stay on another semester to make them up while concentrating on the others now. I would strongly suggest they talk it over with each other and think of the implications of the alternatives. In saying this, I would be keeping in mind, the part of the underachievement syndrome which says he may be doing this failing work as part of acting out against the parents. Then I would make sure my last comment would repeat the urge to have David come back or go somewhere for counseling.

The values of the counselor are involved in so far as the counselor feels that he has the right to make such a decision for others and how much he values staying in school. A counselor who thinks staying in school is all important will let this influence his discussion with the father. There is also the question of whether or not the counselor feels the father should be involved at all, and only talk to the son.

I tried not to let my values come in but still think some are necessary."

The counselor is interested in how the father feels. He indicates that the decision isn't the counselor's, but one that lies with the family. Then the counselor goes and lists a number of alternatives. The counselor notes the question of values, and his role in them. This answer is weak in the sense that the counselor really did not articulate how he personally feels about the value question. It is particularly strong, however, in the explication to the father of the contingencies. Scoring: *Role,* 3; *Options,* 1; *Consistency,* 3; and *Values,* 4.

The most deceptive type of response is that by the counselor who indicates that the student's concerns are of critical importance and that his counselor's role is to advise, yet consistently acts in such a way as to counteract this. Such an example is provided by the following:

"I would reply that this matter was a serious and important one and could not be determined without much consideration. I would reply that I could not make any suggestions at this time and would invite him to make an appointment to see me (with his son, if his son would agree) or to telephone me after I could give it more consideration, and after I discussed it more fully with the son.

(1) This kind of situation may move the counselor to want to make a decision for this boy. The boy should make his own decision after having the counselor help him get the problem in proper perspective, so that he can see it realistically and consider the alternatives.
(2) I would represent the value that the boy should make his own decision; to decide, after weighing alternatives, whether or not to drop out of school.

My loyalty would be toward the boy and any relationship with the
father would take into consideration this loyalty and responsibility
toward my client."

The counselor begins by saying that the matter is important, and that he
could not make any suggestions at this time without further consideration. After
the counselor has given it more consideration, the implication is he will talk
with the father. Again our counselor said this kind of situation may make a counselor want to make a decision for the boy but the boy should make his own decision. Yet the counselor just contradicted himself by saying that he had not
made up his own mind. While he says he represents a value that the boy should
make up his own mind, he himself has already accepted a role in the locus of
responsibility. He says his loyalty would be toward the boy, but has not identified what that loyalty is designed to achieve. Scoring: *Role,* 4; *Options,* 6;
Consistency, 7; and *Values,* 4.

Some counselors can't make up their minds what their role is, or how to be-
have in the counseling session. Such ambivalence of position cannot help but be
translated into behavior.

A counselor with such a dilemma wrote the following:

"Tell his father:

(1) He is failing.
(2) He is so far behind that passing would indeed be difficult.
(3) Before agreeing that he should withdraw you would like to explore
    with David:
    (a) His choice of major—why did he leave all the requirements
        go until one semester? Why did he do better in the earlier
        semesters? It is possible that it was because he took fewer
        science courses?
    (b) Why did he wait until he couldn't . . . possibly catch up
        to come for help? Is it a possibility that he wanted to drop out
        of school and helped manufacture an excuse? If so, why?
(4) After settling these matters with David, then perhaps it would be
    better for him to withdraw for the semester—re-entering at a later
    date with a new major, or whatever was found to be necessary.

Does it necessarily bring *my* values into play? David and his father's
values in regard to education, failures, etc. will definitely be involved,
but will mine? In framing an answer to the father my main concern
will have to be what is best for David, not his father, etc. My answer
may also have to reflect school policy, but I'm still not sure my values, or
the school's values, would be an issue, and what David values and his
father values, I cannot say at this point."

This counselor would have himself indicating the son is failing, and that passing would be difficult. The counselor then says that before agreeing that the son should withdraw, he'd like to talk more with the son. He has almost put himself in a position of agreeing and disagreeing with the choice.

The counselor wonders whether or not his values come into play. He's already brought them into play by indicating that he has the opportunity to agree. The counselor says that in framing an answer, his concern is what's best for the student. The counselor then reverses himself by saying his answer may also have to reflect school policy. He then adds to his own confusion by saying "I'm still not sure my values or the school's values would be an issue." Perhaps his only intelligent statement was in the last sentence where he said "what David and his father values, I cannot say at this point." Scoring: *Role,* 5; *Options,* 5; *Consistency,* 6; and *Values,* 6.

NAME INDEX

Abeles, N., 7, 79, 94
Adams, H. E., 87
Adams, H. F., 71
Allen, Gay Wilson, 4
Allen, T., 58, 59, 69, 77, 96, 118
Allport, G. W., 41, 42, 77, 93
Anderson, C. C., 18-19
Arbuckle, D. S., 7

Baer, D., 120, 122, 124
Bailey, D. E., 77, 118
Bakan, D., 74
Barron, F., 68
Barry, R., 6
Berg, I. A., 87
Bergin, A. E., 5, 11
Bergman, D., 98
Betz, B. J., 6
Biddle, Bruce J., 18
Bieri, J., 22
Bijou, S. W., 122, 124
Blocher, D. H., 39
Bloom, B., 8, 109
Blum, G. S., 71, 72
Bordin, E. S., 39, 40, 44, 75, 97
Bowler, E. M., 6
Brams, J. M., 7, 12
Brayfield, A. H., 41
Bronfenbrenner, U., 41, 74, 75
Broudy, I. F., 94
Bruner, J., 41, 68, 75
Butler, M. M., 81

Campbell, R. E., 7
Carkhuff, R. R., 6, 11, 81, 119
Cartwright, D. S., 97
Cattell, R. B., 11
Cooley, William W., 31
Cottle, W. C., 7
Cox, R. D., 6
Crites, J. O., 32
Cronbach, L. J., 59, 73, 110
Crowne, D., 88, 89
Cutler, R. L., 72-73, 74

Danskin, D. B., 7
Dawson, F. T., 6
Descartes, R., 122, 124
DeForest, Izette, 5

Continued
Dellis, N. P., 75
Desroches, H. F., 88
Dickenson, W. A., 117, 119
Dole, A. A., 8
Dollard, J., 68, 69
Domas, S. J., 18
Dudek, S. Z., 9, 10, 24
Dymond, R. F., 71

Edwards, A. L., 89
Ellsworth, S., 5, 78, 93
Emlaw, R., 24, 53, 62
Erikson, E., 122, 124
Eron, L. D., 101
Eysenck, H. J., 87, 117

Farber, I. E., 122, 124
Fattu, Nicholas A., 18
Feder, D. S., 67
Feld, S., 5
Fenichel, O., 70, 76
Ferenczi, 5
Fiedler, F. E., 5, 94, 95, 97
Finesinger, J., 58, 103
Fiske, D. W., 8, 94, 118
Fliess, R., 75, 76, 77
Frank, G. H., 97, 98
Frank, J. D., 5
Frenkel-Brunswik, E., 71
Freud, S., 70

Gardner, R., 22, 91
Getzels, J. W., 18, 19, 68, 69
Gilbreath, S. H., 117
Gill, N., 76
Goldberger, L., 90
Goldstein, L., 79
Goodlad, John I., 18
Graves, G. T., 6
Green, G. H., 71
Greenson, R. R., 75,76
Guilford, J. P., 18, 110
Gurin, G., 5

Hahn, M. E., 5
Halkides, G., 80-81
Hartman, 41
Hartmann, H., 70

187

SUBJECT INDEX

192